Discovering God
in the Ordinary

FOUR WOMEN. DIFFERENT JOURNEYS.
SAME PURSUIT.

LuAnn Adams
Heidi Lee Anderson
Jo Bender
Julie Miller

Heart Matters
PUBLISHING CO. LLC

DISCOVERING GOD IN THE ORDINARY: FOUR WOMEN. DIFFERENT JOURNEYS. SAME PURSUIT©2017

Published by Heart Matters Publishing, P.O. Box 10671, St. Paul, Minnesota 55110

ISBN #: 978-1-365-39979-4

CONTENTS

Discovering Love

Discovering Wisdom

Discovering Faith

Discovering How to Let Go

Discovering Our Worth

Discovering Prayer and Solitude

Discovering Our Blind Spots

Discovering the Blessing of Friendship

Discovering God in Celebrations

DEDICATION

To the One who spoke these thoughts into our
hearts...we humbly lift our gratitude to You.
May this book bring You glory.

To our dear families who are gifts from
heaven itself. Thank you for your love and
support.

INTRODUCTION

Do you ever find yourself waiting for God to show up?

So often we think that the spiritual life happens in cathedrals and on mission trips, during prayer services or at funerals, as if faith has a proper place in which it is supposed to reside. But the truth is that much of the time you and I are surrounded by moments of faith—right in the midst of our very ordinary lives. Perhaps your faith perks up in the recognition of a beautiful sunset. Maybe God makes himself known while you're sitting in the drop-off line at your child's school, or in the checkout line at the local grocery store. Perhaps you feel most connected to God when you're connecting with others—be it in meeting a friend for coffee or in holding hands with your husband.

Faith is not to be pigeon-holed as a Sunday-only experience, but is rather practiced as we go through our daily lives, recognizing Jesus as a part of those ordinary tasks. Catching sight of these moments where God is not only present but active has the power to change the way we see the world around us. Discovering God in both the exciting and the mundane changes the way we think about ourselves, as being clearly identified as a person worthy of his presence. It takes being intentional. It takes looking beyond our ordinary circumstances and into the beckoning eyes of our extraordinary Lord. Sometimes we have to work to see him, and other times his face is clear as day. But this much is true. He *is* with us. Always.

As you read some of our stories, it is our sincere hope that you will catch a glimpse of yourself in some of the writings, and thereby catch a glimpse of God's gentle presence in the stories he is writing for you.

Blessings on your journey.

LuAnn, Heidi, Jo and Julie

Discovering Love

Gushing Over Your Spouse

Heidi

Let everything you say be good and helpful,
so that your words will be an encouragement
to those who hear them.
—Ephesians 4:29

Ever opened up a love letter that didn't belong to you? Whether it was an old note you found in your mom's journal or a message you were supposed to pass along to your best friend in the 7th grade, curiosity got the best of you, and you couldn't help but read it.

When we open up Song of Songs, we may have similar feelings. Solomon is the author of this dramatic love story, and as he records his pursuit, their courtship, and finally his marriage to the Shulamite maiden, he leaves little detail to the imagination. Right out of the gate, both the beloved and her lover talk a lot about what they love about each other:

> *How pleasing is your fragrance; your name is like the spreading fragrance of scented oils. (1:3)*

> *How beautiful you are, my darling, how beautiful! Your eyes are like doves. You are so handsome, my love, pleasing beyond words! (1:15-16)*

It doesn't end there either. Flip a few pages over and the compliments just get more detailed, more passionate, and more…unique.

Your eyes are like doves behind your veil. Your hair falls in waves, like a flock of goats winding down the slopes of Gilead. Your teeth are as white as sheep, recently shorn and freshly washed. Your smile is flawless, each tooth matched with its twin. Your lips are like scarlet ribbon; your mouth is inviting. Your cheeks are like rosy pomegranates behind your veil. Your neck is as beautiful as the tower of David, jeweled with the shields of a thousand heroes. (4:1-4)

It's easy to dismiss this kind of obsession with naïve, young love—maybe it's simply infatuation. I mean, didn't every couple start off this way? All googly-eyed, head-over-heels, hopelessly-devoted-to-you kind of a feeling? Just give them a couple decades, even a couple years, and things will surely fizzle down, right? She'll load the dishwasher wrong, he'll leave the cupboards open. She'll put on a few pounds, he'll get caught up in his work. And kids? That'll be the icing on the cake. Passion dissolved. Fascination redirected. And the warm fuzzies nowhere to be found.

But is that true? What if there was a way to keep the flame going? What if God has already shown us clues to keep a relationship strong? What if, through the Song of Songs, he is showing us a better way, a more loving way?

One theme to notice from start to finish—starting with the courtship (1:1-3:5), moving onto the wedding (3:6-5:1), and then beyond throughout their maturing marriage (5:2-8:14)—there is no shortness of affirmation. Both the lover and her beloved heap on the compliments, gush over their adorations, and say every good thing that crosses their mind.

How often do we do that with our spouses and loved ones? When they're having a good hair day, do we say so? Or just move onto the next subject? When they've been working tirelessly at work, do we exhort their determination or complain about the time away? When they've done the laundry, do we go out of our way to say thanks or just take it for granted?

> *Kind words are like honey—sweet to the soul and healthy for the body. (Proverbs 16:24)*

> *So, encourage each other and build each other up, just as you are already doing. (1 Thessalonians 5:11)*

We are human beings that were made to hear and speak words of affirmation. But this world isn't known for its pat on the backs and standing ovations. Instead, it's filled with criticism, strong opinions, and quick judgments. So, the question is, if we don't speak love, who will?

Who will first look outward when it's so much easier to look inward? Who will give the standing ovations when their spouse's meeting rooms, gyms, or concert halls are quiet as a mouse? Who will speak up, clap, dish out bold praise, and shout out congrats when their spouse is feeling insecure or stressed out? Or do you think your spouse values awkward silence, a thankless job, or the doubt that comes from never really hearing praise?

These lovebirds from the Song of Songs showered each other with praise—and it wasn't because they were naïve, young, ignorant, or simple-minded. Even in the final chapters of Song of Songs, we see a matured marriage; yet, their language was no different from when they first started dating. This may be the clue we've been searching for, the way to restore bitterness or resentment, and the key to a healthy, strong marriage.

We may not need to go to the extent to tell our spouse that their feet are like bases of pure gold, their waist like a mound of wheat, and their cheeks like beds of spice. But it wouldn't take much to say, "I love you" or "You look great today;" and it certainly wouldn't hurt to hear, "I'm proud to be your spouse." Maybe a kind word is all it would take to signal those warm fuzzies back again.

And who knows, maybe Solomon's pick-up lines *do* work, and in that case, they just might like hearing that their rounded thighs are like jewels and their nose like a tower. It's your call if you want to try it out.

Regardless what the compliment may be today, let's take the example of God's Word, and if we're thinking something good, why don't we try saying it out loud too?

What is one piece of affirmation I can speak out loud to my spouse this week?

A Sacred Romance

Julie

Mary's heart began to thump and her hands to shake a little in her delight and excitement. What was this under her hands which was square and made of iron and which her finger found a hole in?

It was the lock of the door which had been closed ten years and she put her hand in her pocket, drew out the key and found it fitted the keyhole. She put the key in and turned it. It took two hands to do it, but it did turn.

And then she took a long breath and looked behind her up the long walk to see if anyone was coming. No one was. No one ever did come, it seemed, and she took another long breath, because she could not help it, and she held back the swinging curtain of ivy and pushed back the door which opened slowly—slowly.

Then she slipped through it, and shut it behind her, and stood with her back against it, looking about her and breathing quite fast with excitement, and wonder, and delight.

She was standing inside *the secret garden.*

It was the sweetest, most mysterious-looking place anyone could imagine.

—Frances Hodgson Burnett

There's something quite delicious about discovering a secret place.

My uncle once discovered a hidden little cove on one of his many *Huckleberry Finn* adventures along the riverbanks of the

Allegheny. This sweet secluded pocket of still, clear water was where he would bring my sis and I to swim—while the river itself raced past just feet away. It was our secret place and we, like Mary in her secret garden, felt such incredible awe, wonder and delight when there.

When visiting my hubby's sister and brother-in-law in Morelia, Mexico last February, I discovered another wonderful little secret. Hidden behind the barred gates and stucco exteriors of the houses built one right next to the other were…

Private gardens. Walled-in spaces for the homeowners alone to enjoy. Some were decorated with pavers and fountains, others with grassy areas to lounge in. Each one hidden away from the stares of the people on the street.

Perhaps that's what Solomon envisioned when he wrote the following love letter to his new bride…

> *You have captured my heart, my treasure, my bride.*
>
> *You are my private garden…scented with the very choicest perfumes! An orchard of pomegranates with all kinds of luscious fruit… A secluded spring, a hidden fountain, a well of fresh water…*
>
> —Song of Songs 4:9, 12

Ahh…young love. There's nothing quite like it. Every rendezvous is like a secreting away.

Unfortunately, as time passes, so often does the awe, wonder and delight that accompanies those newly married years.

I know. As a bride, myself, of 38 years, my garden has a tendency to fall into a state similar to what Mary found in the secret garden…

> *The high walls which shut in the garden were covered with the leafless stems of climbing roses, which were so thick*

that they were matted together. All the ground was covered with a grass of wintery brown, and out of it grew clumps of bushes which were surely rose bushes if they were alive. There were neither leaves nor roses on them now, and Mary did not know whether they were dead or alive...

"How still it is!" she whispered.

"No wonder it is still; I am the first person who has spoken in here for ten years."

Like gardens, marriages need tending to. If we aren't proactive, it won't take long for them to fall into disrepair.

I came across a troubling statistic as I was pondering this. According to quora.com, forty percent of all marriages end in divorce within eight years. Just eight short years...before the well of fresh water runs dry and all the garden beds die.

This is sobering. And convicting.

But, reading Solomon's words is convicting on yet another level.

If Solomon's words do indeed have a dual meaning, as most biblical scholars contend, then my heart is a secret garden where God comes calling for me.

> *Arise, come, my darling; my beautiful one, come with me.*
> —Song of Songs 2:13

Mary's heart pounded at the thought of entering in to her secret place. Does my heart share her excitement, wonder and delight? Do I look for as many opportunities as I can find to secret away with my Savior?

Is the garden of my heart exclusively his? Is it a private space where I can rendezvous with him and him alone?

And what of the state of my heart? Is it an inviting place, a place where love permeates every nook and cranny? Where the Savior feels welcomed? Where he has been anticipated? A prepared place filled with pomegranates and a well full of fresh water?

There's something quite delicious about discovering a secret place.

May the garden of our hearts be just that—both in our marriages and in our love relationship with God.

Man's deepest need is to experience the oneness of authentic love in a dependable relationship. We are not to be a garden enclosed locking love out, but a private protected garden for royal use into which we invite our beloved to enter.
—New Spirit-Filled Life Bible

God will rejoice over you as a bridegroom rejoices over his bride.
—Isaiah 62:5

What can I do today to prepare my heart for the Lord?

Scribbles of Love

Jo

*Love always protects, always trusts, always hopes,
always perseveres. Love never fails.*
—1 Corinthians 13:7-8

As I strolled through the greeting card aisle at my favorite Hallmark store, I perused the choices for a Valentines card for my hubby. I repeat the same diatribe in my head each year. Do I go silly or serious? I seem to have many choices…fun and flirty, or sentimental and romantic. Which way will I tell my husband that I love him? And which card do I think will get his attention this year as he walks through the aisle? How will he express his adoration for me?

I am grateful to report that no matter what card my husband chooses for me, it's the words he writes by hand that always speak to my heart. He has a way of reflecting on our current situation, noting both challenging and uplifting events from the previous year, and always concluding that we, he and I, are in this life together, that the seal on this relationship remains firmly affixed in place.

I am grateful for those words. I do not take for granted that he takes the time to write them. But I am especially thankful that he considers each year an opportunity to walk together down this road called marriage. And each time I read the words scribbled on the card, I am reminded of the importance of telling my husband how I truly feel, especially as it applies to love.

The Bible is filled with verses describing both God's love for his people and also how his people are to love others. Maybe your mind goes directly to John 3:16, or 1 Corinthians 13. But when it comes to sharing your heart with your husband, I can't think of a better book than Song of Solomon.

Song of Solomon (or Song of Songs) is a magnificent love poem describing the godly, fervent love between Solomon and his wife. Read a few of the passionate words of a love-sick couple.

She
Let him kiss me with the kisses of his mouth,
for your love is more delightful than wine.
Pleasing is the fragrance of your perfumes;
your name is like perfume poured out.
– Song of Solomon 1:2-3

He
How beautiful you are, my darling!
Oh, how beautiful!
Your eyes are doves.
–Song of Solomon 1:15

She
How handsome you are, my beloved!
Oh, how charming!
And our bed is verdant.
–Song of Solomon 1:16

He
My dove in the clefts of the rock,
in the hiding places on the mountainside,
show me your face,
let me hear your voice;
for your voice is sweet,
and your face is lovely.
–Song of Solomon 2:14

He

As a lily among brambles,
so is my love among the young women.
–Song of Solomon 2:2

She

As an apple tree among the trees of the forest,
so is my beloved among the young men.
With great delight I sat in his shadow,
and his fruit was sweet to my taste.
–Song of Solomon 2:3

It looks like Solomon might support my husband's scribbling on the card and might encourage me to do the same. Expressing our love to our mate might be considered beneficial, encouraging, and even recommended.

Some scholars point to Song of Solomon as a picture of Christ's love for the church. Others say the Song is an allegory of sacred love between God and Israel or Christ and the soul. But many scholars cannot seem to fully push aside the beauty of the Song as *poetry*, a collection of verses celebrating God's gift of love between man and woman. And as you read in this exchange between Solomon and his beloved, there is no question that they aren't holding back their affections for each other.

If that is true, that God's love is a gift for us, then my love for my hubby is a gift I fully receive but strive to not keep. Because every bit I give away, whether in the form of a card, caring words, or loving actions, is simply a reflection of the perfect love that first came from God himself.

So, this year, buy that card—silly or serious—but take a stab at writing your own thoughts too. After all, God wrote a pretty lengthy love letter for all of his people to read.

We can at least participate in sharing that gift with the one we call our beloved.

What words best communicate how I feel about my spouse?
Have I written them down for my beloved to see?

Unloved

LuAnn

*The biggest disease this day and age is that
of people feeling unloved.*
—Princess Diana

Feeling unloved.

We've all been there.

And days like Valentine's Day can intensify those feelings.

Maybe you feel like Cinderella, knowing your Prince Charming is out there somewhere, but you are stuck sitting among the ashes while your friends attend the ball; and unlike Cinderella, you have no fairy godmother.

Or, sometimes worse yet, you think you married Prince Charming, only to find him not quite up to the task. He brings home a Valentines card he hastily bought last minute at the gas station at the same time he picked up his usual coffee; or, he bought you lingerie (which we all know is really *his* gift); or, he forgot you completely...again. As Abhishele Tiwari says, "I'd rather be alone and feel lonely and unloved than be in a relationship and feel the same way."

Maybe you have recently lost love...the love of our life has passed on... You keep trying every day to figure out your new normal, and it is a painful and lonely endeavor.

As I have looked around Perkins on a late morning, I have noted an elderly man or lady sitting alone with their meal; I envision them seeing a shadow of their spouse sitting across the booth, as it once was, when they would talk over trivial or impactful issues they shared.

Or maybe, like too many people I know, the person you loved with abandon, has instead abandoned you.

Wherever you find yourself, dear friend, you are reading this today because God wants to remind you that you are indeed loved. He wants to remind you that he is the true lover of your soul.

In the Song of Solomon (or Song of Songs) we have a beautiful, poetic, portrayal of young love between a man and a woman (The Courtship: 1:2-3:5; The Wedding 3:6-5:1; The Maturing Marriage 5:2-8:14).

However, as with most books in the Old Testament, not only is the story to be read literally to help us understand the precious physical, mental, and emotional love between a man and woman when carried out in the manner God intended, but most early scholars believe it was also to be read allegorically as God's love for us and as a foreshadowing of Christ's love for his people; it also portrays "the intensity of divine love within the human heart" (SparkNotes).

As Ray Stedman states in his article, *A Love Song and a Hymn*, "From the very earliest Christian centuries, this book was taken in that way. Even the Jews took it allegorically... You see, he wasn't singing just a purely human love song. He sang this before Jehovah. This was also a song about his own relationship to God. It was because of this interpretation that this song was such a comfort to the persecuted saints of the Reformation and the post-Reformation periods...and was one of the most read and loved books of all."

Song of Solomon 2:4 reads: "He has taken me to the banquet hall, and his banner over me is love."

In 2:16 it says, "My beloved is mine, and I am his. He feeds his flock among the lilies." Here is a picture of the security of the believer in Christ (John 10:28-29) and the love of the Good Shepherd who lays down his life for us (John 10:11). 7:10 reads similarly, "I am my beloved's, and his desire is towards me." (gotquestions.org)

And because of him, we are no longer stained by sin, having had our spots removed by his blood. (Song of Solomon 4:7 and Ephesians 5:27.)

Stedman also notes, "As you read in this book of the rapturous delight that the bride and the bridegroom experience in one another, you are reading a magnificent and beautiful description of what God intends the relationship to be between himself and each individual." (Also discussed in Ephesians 5.)

The Bible Study Tools website notes that 5:2-8 shows, "Christ's love to us should engage ours to him, even in the most self-denying instances."

It goes on to note that 5:9-16 shows that "Christians, who are well acquainted with Christ themselves, should do all they can to make others know something of him." My twenty-one-year-old daughter lived this out. On Valentine's Day, she texted me trying to find where I was. She caught up with me outside Tousley Sports. She and her good friend jumped out of her car and into the back of our SUV while handing me a beautiful coral-fringed cream rose saying, "Happy Valentine's Day." Then she shared the following:

> "This past week I had an anxiety attack. I tried to find someone to help talk me through. But my roommate was gone, and I couldn't track down any of my friends. I was walking down a college hall, still beside myself, when a girl stopped me and said, 'Would you pray with me? I want to pray with you.'

She pulled me to a corner, and although I don't remember the exact words, she reminded me that God valued and loved me, that he had his Spirit over me and was with me, even in hard times. Then she handed me a rose.

You see, I really struggle with bringing my burdens and anxieties to God and to feel loved by God during those times. I have been wrestling with God about this and asking him to move this head knowledge of his love down to my heart by showing himself to me.

God used this girl to remind me that he is with me, even during these hard times, even during these times I have trouble expressing my need or feeling his presence.

It impacted me so much that I decided on Valentine's day to remind others of his love for them and to hand out a rose as a physical reminder to whomever God leads me to."

We talked for a while longer, and then my daughter and her friend were off to their next rose delivery.

A dear friend of mine who experienced a painful divorce called later fighting tears, "I just wanted you to know that God used your daughter today. I was feeling really down this morning, and she came with a rose and a reminder that God loved me."

So, my dear friend…do you need that reminder that God loves you dearly? If so, I'm following in the steps of my daughter to remind you that God is saying to you: "I love you. You are my beloved."

> *Jesus, Lover of my soul,*
> *Jesus, I will never let you go*
> *You've taken me from the miry clay*
> *You've set my feet upon the Rock, and now I know…*
> —Hillsong

By this the love of God is revealed in us: that God has sent his one and only Son into the world so that we may live through him. In this is love: not that we have loved God, but that he loved us and sent his Son to be the atoning sacrifice for our sins.
—1 John 4:9-10

Do I need to be reminded how much God loves me? Is there anyone in my life that needs to be reminded of God's love?

The One Jesus Loved

Jo

I'm not living for applause, I'm already so adored.
It's all His stage, He knows my name.
—Francesca Battistelli

Some time ago, I attended a track-and-field day for my son. As a volunteer at the long jump station, I filled out a name tag and took my post. For some reason, I simply wrote, "Sam's Mom." Child after child would pass through and they would immediately know that I belonged with that snappy little 3rd grade boy named Sam. We had a connection. Even after the event was through, children would run up to me and say, "Sam's Mom—look at all the ribbons I won!" or "Sam's Mom—can you watch me run?"

Knowing who I belonged to somehow made the kids feel like they knew me. We were buds. My name was not important in that particular context. But my relation to their friend was significant. Furthermore, as Sam's Mom, I saw myself not as a teacher or writer or radio host, but as someone who was there to serve the 3rd graders during their special day.

It reminds me of the gospel writer, John.

In his gospel account, he writes about the unmatched and unparalleled love of God. John has often been described as the beloved disciple. This title is not given as a status symbol—Jesus did not play favorites. Jesus himself does not use this title for John or any other disciple. But rather, *the beloved disciple* was how John described *himself* in the gospel that bears his name.

On at least four occasions, John refers to himself as *the disciple whom Jesus loved.*

Listen in as he describes himself in the following verses...

One of them, *the disciple whom Jesus loved,* was reclining next to him (John 13:23).

Jesus saw his mother and *the disciple whom Jesus loved* standing nearby, and he said to her, "Woman, here is your son" (John 19:26a).

Then *the disciple whom Jesus loved* said to Peter, "It is the Lord!" As soon as Simon Peter heard him say, "It is the Lord," he wrapped his outer garment around him (for he had taken it off) and jumped into the water. (John 21:7)

Peter turned and saw that *the disciple whom Jesus loved* was following them. (John 21:20a)

Perhaps this was John's way of exhibiting remarkable humility. Or, maybe his experience of being loved by Jesus was more precious to him than even his own name. John is said to have had a greater understanding of God's loving nature because he experienced God's love in a distinct way. He knew and experienced this love of God in a way that trumped everything else that he thought about himself. He was no longer just John. He was no longer just a fisherman, a sinner, a disciple-in-training or a flawed human being. His identity no longer came from what he did or didn't do, but came from the One who knew all of these things about him, and yet loved him fully anyway. John based his identity in relation to Christ. He simply saw himself as *the one whom Jesus loved.*

Imagine how our life might look different if we started from this assumption. *I am the one whom Jesus loves.* And as such, our worthiness would already be established. Our status would already be decided. We might pray differently or act differently toward our neighbors. We might love others with the same love he bestows on us.

He knows me.

He sees me.

And he *still* loves me.

I am the one whom Jesus loves.

When we think of ourselves this way, we begin to read Scripture differently. It is no longer for those people of that time. Each verse is written with us in mind. Imagine this paraphrase of John 3:16:

> *For God so loved [your name] that he gave his only son, that since [your name] believes in him, [your name] shall not perish but [your name] shall have eternal life.*

The Bible is personal. It's God's love letter to us. We are the ones whom Jesus loves.

How about putting that on your next nametag?

Am I able to fully grasp how much I am loved by my heavenly Father?

Stumbling, Bumbling, Fumbling

Julie

We pay a heavy price for our fear of failure. It is a powerful obstacle to growth. There is no learning without some difficulty and fumbling. If you want to keep on learning, you must keep on risking failure all your life.
—John W. Gardner

We started months in advance of our trip to France checking out French CD's from the library. It had been 34 years since we had lived there, and sadly, without constant use, much of our French had been forgotten. So, we listened to CD's at home and in our cars, repeating the words and sentences like a couple of mina birds. My hubby practiced every chance he had with a French grad student at the U. And I pulled my old book, *French for Le Snob: Adding Panache to Your Everyday Conversations* off the shelf and studied it like I was preparing for an exam.

But, for all of my preparation, I still ended up stumbling, bumbling and fumbling my way through conversations.

It wasn't that I couldn't understand what most folks were saying. My struggle occurred when I tried to enter into a discussion. The perfectionist in me would get so preoccupied trying to remember the past, present and future tenses of words and sentence structures that by the time I had my thoughts formulated, the topic had long passed and was onto another. That left me no other recourse but to smile and nod a lot, and rely on my hubby, Rey, who has such adeptness to languages, to carry the conversation for me.

But, it was frustrating. We women have at least 10,000 words a day we have to get off our chests. I knew I couldn't keep this up forever.

So, I began praying, "O God, remember in Acts 2:4, 6-8 where the disciples were all filled with the Holy Spirit and began to speak in other languages? And the people who heard them were mystified, surprised and amazed, saying, *'Look, aren't all these folks Galileans? How is it then that they can speak in our native tongues?'* Well, I'm just wondering if you would be willing to do that for me too?!"

What I sensed God whispering to my heart instead was this, "I know that you think that a supernatural dose of French language skills is what you need most right now, but, what I long to do will stretch and grow you. So, instead of supernatural French skills, I would like to fill you with a fresh dose of supernatural *love* for these, my precious ones, here in France. My love can overcome any language barrier."

The next morning Rey went to work making cheese at the Fruitière de La Chapelle d'Abondance. As I stepped out onto our deck overlooking sweeping views of the French Alps, I decided then and there that, weak language skills and all, I was going to get to know this sweet little alpine town and love on the folks who call it home.

It was the most difficult week I've had in some time. But, it was also a blessing that I shall not easily forget. Without my crutch (Rey) to lean on, I made friends with the gals at the boulangerie (bakery) and bumbled my way through conversations with folks I met as I puttered through little shops and snapped pictures of their beautiful little Ville.

The love God planted in my heart that week blossomed friendships everywhere we went as a result.

But, you don't need to travel the globe to experience love's beautiful gifts of friendship. Every day we have an opportunity to love folks right where they live: folks, which for all intents and purposes "speak a different language" than we do. Imagine what God could do if we were filled with a supernatural love for folks who think differently, act differently, and live differently than we do?

Sweetest Savior, thank you that despite all my fumbling efforts at communication, your love sown deep in my heart for my French brothers and sisters bloomed friendships impossible without it. May I carry that love for others henceforth with whomever I meet...for they are dearly loved by You.

Love will find its way through all languages on its own.
—Rumi

Love each other as I have loved you.
—John 15:12

Who can I show love to this week?

Putting Shame to Bed

Jo

To be a Christian means to forgive the inexcusable because God has forgiven the inexcusable in you.
—C.S. Lewis

Big crocodile tears formed in the eyes of my youngest as he stood in the doorway of my bedroom about an hour after I'd already put him to bed for the night.

"What's wrong?" I asked, "Did you have a bad dream?"

He said, through the tears, that he had forgotten about a project that was due tomorrow. He was supposed to provide some supplies. He'd forgotten…and now he would never get it done on time. Sobbing now, my boy buried his little head in my shoulder as I tried to tell him that it would be okay.

I finally got out of him that what he needed was some "insulation" for a solar house he was building. Newspaper, bubble wrap, or Styrofoam would work, he said. I've learned from previous late-night homework mishaps that it seems to work better to just hunker down and get the work done before the head hits the pillow. Otherwise, getting to sleep proves to be a challenge.

So, we rummaged around the basement for a few minutes and settled on an old TV box that contained some Styrofoam. He was elated to find that my basement storage room contained many treasures. Truth be told, I could have probably provided Styrofoam for the entire class.

We packed up a grocery bag full of the "insulation," and put it by the back door. I brought my son upstairs to tuck him in and held him long enough to feel that he was still shaking, and although he was exhausted, he wasn't ready to let me go. I wasn't ready to let go either.

"Why are you still shaking, honey?" I asked. "You are all set for the morning, and we did it in five minutes. Now you can sleep and tomorrow's a new day."

"Mom," he said, "I should have done better."

I asked him if he happened to remember what I used to tell him when he was a wee little boy of two or three years. It's a phrase I used to purposely repeat over and over to make sure my boys knew that my love for them was not based on performance or good behavior or mood.

"Do you remember what I always said to you when you were little?" I asked, just hoping it had sunk in… just hoping he had written those words on his heart.

"Yes Mom. You'd say, 'nothing I can do will make you love me any less.'"

And in that instant, I was transported back to the times I'd had this same talk with him after he'd done something not-so good, like coloring all over the walls with my brand new permanent marker, or sneaking downstairs in the middle of the night to eat the left-over birthday cake and leaving a frosting trail right back to his room. I remember catching him in little lies and bigger calamities, like when he hurt his brother or hurt me with his words. And I remember the embarrassment on his face, not just because he'd gotten caught, but because he knew he'd disappointed me. Those same crocodile tears…that same burying of the head…that same shame.

And those same words. I meant them now just like I meant them then.

"Nothing you can do will ever make me love you less. Nothing."

I tell my boys this even when I don't feel like it, when part of me would rather let them stew in their shame for a while before I offer that hug. Especially those times I tell them, "Nothing you can do will make me love you any less. Nothing."

I tell them this because God tells me this. Every. Single. Day. He doesn't hesitate when I forget to act Christ-like toward people who wrong me. He doesn't waver when I forget to spend time with him. He doesn't withhold his love when I use my words as daggers that hurt instead of as words that heal. He doesn't hesitate when I wrong my neighbor or my husband or myself. He picks up my face in his hands and whispers, "Nothing you can do will make me love you less. Nothing."

I envision this type of treatment when Jesus encountered so many, like the woman caught in adultery who was crumpled in a heap on the ground. Once the accusers had left, I envision Jesus going to her, reaching down, and lifting her head so that their faces are close. Her eyes are looking down at the ground but he keeps repeating something like, "Look here, child. Nothing you can do will make me love you less. Nothing."

I envision Jesus doing the same to Peter, his disciple, who had spent the better part of three years traveling with, and learning from Jesus during his public ministry. This same Peter, who denied even knowing Jesus the night the crowds sentenced him to death. I can't imagine the disappointment Jesus must have felt to watch what he foretold come to fruition. Yet, when Jesus returned to Peter three days later, he didn't let his friend stew in his shame. Quite the opposite. While the Bible doesn't give us all the details, I envision Jesus reaching down and lifting Peter's head so that their faces are close and repeating those same words, "Look here, friend. Nothing you can do will make me love you less. Nothing."

I continue to stumble, but God continues to lift my head too. And yet, I forget. Day-after-day, I find myself asking for forgiveness for the same things that I tried to tell God I would try not to do again. Why is it so hard to remember the simple fact that while we might be flawed and while we might forget, our God is so secure in his love for us that there is truly nothing that we can do that would ever take that love away?

As I tuck in my son, I ask him, "Would you like me to stay a while?" He says, "No Mom. I'm okay now. Thank you for reminding me."

The next morning when I rustle him out of bed, he opens his eyes and that same glimmer reappears. It is as if nothing happened the night before. He flashes that smile that says, "I know I'm loved," and my heart melts, for I know it too.

And as I give him a little hug and send him off to the bus, I pray a little prayer of thankfulness that God has given me these boys so that I can learn this lesson again for myself.

As I turn to go inside, I see it…the grocery bag of Styrofoam… sitting by the back door.

Oh well…time for another reminder.

Knowing God always forgives, how can I best approach others who have wronged me?

Discovering Wisdom

Folly and Friends

LuAnn

*A friend is someone who knows the song in your heart and can
sing it back to you when you have forgotten the words.*
–Unknown

I had only left them alone for a few minutes. But, as I walked
back into the kitchen, there sat little Alyssa in the exer-saucer,
her face sporting some new vibrant colors. The two culprits were
nowhere to be found. When I did locate the giggling girls, they
wore finger paint "make-up" as well; the nice white paper that
was supposed to display their bold paint, glared back, empty.

Doing day care, I never wanted to leave these two gals together
unattended for very long. Ever. One was my daughter,
McKayla. She and the other girl, Tara, equaled high energy, out-
of-the-box thinking, and when they were together, the fireworks
they each created, seemed to more than double in intensity.

One day they decided Mc's curtains looked like a fun Tarzan
rope… That didn't go so well.

Another time they decided to empty every sunscreen I owned
onto the slide in our backyard to increase sliding speed… That
didn't go so well either.

McKayla's younger brother, Austin, and Tara's younger sister,
Alyssa, were their "dolls;" thankfully they came out in one piece
through all of Mc's and Tara's escapades. (Conversely, Austin
and Alyssa's idea of a roaring good time was reading together.)

Friends definitely influence us. We influence our friends.

When my daughter got older, her friend choices became a more serious matter.

She was often drawn to people who had a good heart, but, who tended to make unwise choices and didn't have much direction from home. "I know I can help them, mom," she would say.

She had to learn that, although her heart was doing the right thing, her methodology was unwise; she learned that keeping a wise friend or two close by had to be priority, as well as not hanging with certain friends in certain situations or for long periods of time.

Wise King Solomon, in passing down wisdom to his children and others in the book of Proverbs, knew how important it was to address the topic of friends. He understood the influence our friends can have on us:

> *Walk with wise people and become wise; befriend fools and get in trouble.* (13:20, CEB)

> *Don't hang out with angry people; don't keep company with hotheads. Bad temper is contagious—don't get infected.* (22:24-25, MSG)

> *The godly are cautious in friendship.* (12:26a, NLT)

> *There are "friends" who destroy each other, but a real friend sticks closer than a brother.* (18:24, NLT)

Wise advice. I think we can all think of times when friends talked us into doing extremely foolish things. We can probably even think of a time when we talked our friends into doing something foolish as well.

Many of us have had to learn the hard way how important integrity, wisdom, and love are in our closest friendships.

Because of our friendship experiences, it isn't any wonder we are concerned for our children's friends.

Our children's friends can be a touchy subject with them, however.

I remember when I was a junior in high school sharing my concerns one evening with my mom about some of the choices certain friends were making. "Well, you may need to get a new set of friends," she said. I remember becoming angry. "I've invested years into these friendships, and now you're telling me I'm just supposed to walk away?"

Conversations with my own daughter didn't always go much better.

Although our children usually don't want our advice, they will often listen to our stories. Jesus often taught in story, and it can be a wise venue for us to use as well. Encouraging them to read Proverbs is not a bad idea either.

And then of course, our most mighty influence on our children's friends is prayer. When my children were in school, I was a part of Moms in Prayer groups (formerly MIT), and friends was one of the most often-prayed petitions for our children.

One of the Scriptures we prayed over our children was, "That (child's name) will enjoy the companionship of those who love the Lord and have pure hearts." (II Timothy 2:22b, TLB)

Stormie Omaritian, author of, *The Power of a Praying Parent*, one of my favorite books when my children were young, has this to say:

> *I have always prayed for my children's friends and, for the most part, they've had great ones. Occasionally they've made friends that, as a parent, I had reservations about. Not because I didn't like them... What I didn't like was the type of influence they were on my child, and what the combination of that child and mine produced. The way I always handled this situation was to pray. I prayed for that*

child to be changed or else be taken out of my child's life. In every case that prayer was answered.

I can reiterate having the same experience. Some of my daughter's friends that concerned me left her life; others turned towards God. My daughter learned to be wiser in the area of friends and even how to be a better friend herself.

I can also share that there were times I prayed for God to change *my heart* towards my daughters' friends, and he did. What was once annoyance with a friend was replaced with love; these "rough" friends became precious to me, and I was able to invest in them.

Another friend issue that is hard for parents to watch is when our children are friendless. This, too, is a matter of great prayer. Stormie had this happen to her children when they moved, and it tore her heart to see how lonely they were; I'm sure many of you can relate. She says, *"I often lay awake at night praying on their behalf. There was nothing else I could do. And even if there was, I never would have done as good a job as God did in answer to my prayers. Eventually people came into their lives who have become some of the greatest friends they've ever had."*

I love Stormie's prayer on friends below. Praying this or similar over our children is powerful. And if we find ourselves as an adult going through tough friendship issues, many of the principles can be prayed over ourselves as well.

Lord, I lift up _____ to you and ask that you would bring godly friends and role models into his/her life. Give him/her the wisdom he/she needs to choose friends who are godly and help him/her to never compromise his/her walk wit you in order to gain acceptance. Give me Holy Spirit-inspired discernment in how I guide or influence him/her in the selection of friends. I pray that you would take anyone who is not a godly influence out of his/her life or else transform that person into your likeness.

Your Word says, "He who walks with the wise will be wise, but the companion of fools will be destroyed (Prov. 13:20)." Don't let my child be a companion of fools. Enable him/her to walk with wise friends and not have to experience the destruction that can happen by walking with foolish people. Deliver him/her from anyone with an ungodly character so he/she will not learn that person's ways and set a snare for his/her own soul.

Whenever there is grief over a lost friendship, comfort him/her and send new friends with whom he/she can connect, share and be the person you created him/her to be. Take away any loneliness or low self-esteem that would cause him/her to seek out less than God-glorifying relationships.

In Jesus' name, I pray that you would teach him/her the meaning of true friendship. Teach him/her how to be a good friend and make strong, close, lasting relationships. May each of his/her friendships always glorify you.

What do I value most in my friends? What do my friends value in me?

Guard Your Heart

Julie

And every day, the world will drag you by the hand,
yelling, "This is important! And this. And this…"
And each day, it's up to you to yank your hand back,
put it on your heart and say, "No. This is what's important."
—Iain Thomas

Above all else, guard your heart, for from it
flows the issues of life.
—Proverbs 4:23

When my hubby and I lived in France long years ago, there was an ancient city that I *so* wanted to visit. A city we'd driven past on several occasions. But, we were always on our way to or from a basketball game. And, much to my regret, we never found the time to stop.

Last summer I finally got to check that visit off my bucket list.

Carcassonne is an old fortified city that stands like a beacon on a hilltop. A fairy tale, Cinderella city with turrets and barbicans and stone-laid streets that, if you closed your eyes and imagined it, you would feel quite certain that a horse-mounted knight-in-shining-armor would clip clop past you at any moment.

As romantic as it was to imagine life in those days, God had a few thoughts of his own to speak into my soul that day. Starting with a whispered, *"Guard your heart…"*

I had loved those words from Proverbs ever since I first heard them many years ago. But, being reminded of them again in such an imposing city like Carcassonne, made the words spring to life for me.

The city itself is well over 2,000 years old. In fact, most scholars believe it to have been established around the year 100 BC.

History tells of a King Pepin the Short, who had conquered most of France during his reign. But, in the end he could not penetrate the impregnable fortress of Carcassonne. To this day, it is still protected by its two outer walls and 53 watchtowers.

Walking between those two massive walls, I couldn't help but think about a man in the Bible who knew a thing or two about building walls like these. Nehemiah. He wrote this about his experience…

> *So, we rebuilt the wall till all of it reached half its height, for the people worked with all their heart. Our enemies plotted together to come and fight and stir up trouble. But we prayed to our God and posted a guard day and night to meet this threat.*
>
> *I devoted myself to the work on the wall. The enemy continued his schemes. They tried to frighten us, but I prayed, "Strengthen my hands."*
>
> *So, the wall was completed. Our enemies were defeated, realizing that it had been done with the help of our God.*
> —Nehemiah 4:6, 8; 5:14; 6:2, 9, 15

As I swept my fingertips along one of those thick stone walls, I wondered, "How well am I guarding my heart from outer influences that seek to stir up trouble in my life? What sneaks in when my guard is down? Scepticism? Cynicism? Doubt? Fear?"

I lifted my thoughts heavenward, "Lord, please help me post a guard day and night to meet this threat."

Thoughts of guards caused my eyes to turn upwards toward the tall, commanding watchtowers where many of them would have been stationed. It looked to be quite a climb, but Rey and I decided it would be worth it to wind our way up to the top of one of them.

When we reached the top, we could see for miles. We had a bird's-eye view.

Nothing could've escaped the eyes of a watchman up in this post...unless he wasn't paying attention or paid no heed at all.

As I thought about that, I was reminded of a dialogue that happened between Ezekiel and God that went something like this...

> Ezekiel: *"What if the guard sees the enemy coming, but doesn't blow the trumpet?"*
>
> God: *"Since that guard didn't warn the people...he will be held responsible for whatever disaster befalls them. You, son of man, are the watchman!"*
> —Ezekiel 33:6-7

"*You*...are the watchman!"

I put my hand to my heart as I stood looking over the wide landscape. What a visual God had given me. I am the watchman of my heart. God will hold me responsible for what I let into it and what I don't. If I choose to ignore or disregard those things that lay siege against it, if I fail to keep it undefiled by sin or undisturbed by trouble, I can also expect, as watchmen in Ezekiel's day did, painful consequences to follow.

That's because our hearts are dear to God. When he knit us together in our mother's womb (Psalm 139:13), he not only created our bodies, he shaped our souls...our inner being...who we are down deep…what we think, how we feel and respond. All that is who we are *at heart*.

That's why it is so important that we keep our hearts safe just as we would a precious jewel.

The reason we guard our hearts is because *from it flows the issues of life.* The issues of life—our actions, works, pursuits, and dreams—all proceed from the heart (Pr. 4:23; Matt. 6:21; 12:34; 15:18). When a heart is well-kept it will flow fresh with life-giving healing and wholeness not only to us, but, it will bring solace to others, and more importantly, bring glory to the God who made us.

As Rey and I wandered into the center of Carcassonne, we discovered a large church. Its towers, too, reached skyward. It dawned on me as I stood under its lofty ceiling, that the folks who built this city understood, as Nehemiah had, that beyond their own strength and resolve, beyond any wall or tower they could build, God was their most important ally.

By placing God in the heart of the city, it was a constant reminder to them that they had an infinitely more valuable resource at their disposal. They had prayer. They had a precious friend and Savior they could turn to when they were under attack. A heavenly Father who would hear them when they called for his aid and move on their behalf.

Diligently keeping our hearts *in touch with God* through prayer is vital to thwarting the enemy's schemes. With his help, any outside influences that seek our undoing will be defeated and, as in Nehemiah's life, others will see how precious God is.

The sun was setting as Rey and I walked under the last archway out of Carcassonne. And there, God had one final love gift waiting for me: a stone cross. I stopped to bow my head in prayer, grateful that God had whispered *his heart* to mine that day.

It should be because it is so determinative of every aspect of life. It ultimately determines our love for God and for others. It determines who we are and what we do.

—Unknown

How well am I guarding my heart? Is the condition of my heart my greatest concern?

Wrong Turns

LuAnn

I am the Lord your God who teaches you what is best for you, who directs you in the way you should go. If only you had paid attention to my commands your peace would have been like a river, your righteousness like the waves of the sea.
—Isaiah 48:17-18

It was our annual girls' getaway. A time when we could work on our photo albums and creative memories without interruption from our families.

This time I had traded in a timeshare for a place in the deep woods of Wisconsin. As my van rumbled over the windy, snow-covered hills, we finally found the place after many missed turns.

The building was hugged by trees and hills with no other manmade structures in sight. And not only was it secluded…it was empty. We were the only ones with beating hearts on the premise except for a lady who worked part-time in a tiny front office.

Although the place was nicely kept, it definitely was a throwback. There was only one phone at this resort. It was found in the common area, nestled among the racquet ball courts, pool, hot tub, and ping pong table, any of which we enjoyed whenever we felt the urge to emerge from our photo heaps and cranked-up motivational music.

One day we were returning from a bowling venture in a nearby town, having gotten a tad claustrophobic at the resort, the city gals that we were. Lori and I were talking in the front seat of the van, when our friend Julie calmly poked her blonde head between ours from the seat behind us and said, "Ummmm, ladies, we are heading right towards a lake."

What?!

Sure enough, I had just crested the top of a hill when several yards in front of me was a lake, and I was heading straight towards it. I slammed on the breaks, and we silently looked at the cold, lapping water in front of us for a moment. Once we realized we were safe, we laughed for quite a while. How did that happen?! Where were the warning signs? How could a main road end in a lake?!

We had gotten lost. Very lost. You'd think we would have learned our lesson...

But, after a late dinner out, we once again found ourselves looking in the dark for the right road to take back to the resort. Lori and I figured this one road must be the right one. Julie sitting behind us tried to talk us out of it, but we didn't listen. After a few minutes, she said, "Really, ladies? Our place is desolate, but at least you don't need a machete to clear it out first." Lori and I looked at each other sheepishly. She was right. The road surface was quickly disappearing the further in we went, being swallowed up by wild fern, weeds, and decaying wood. And turning around and getting back out turned out to be quite challenging.

The following day we were driving back from shopping. Lori and I were once again chatting in the front seat. Julie, from the seat behind us called out once again, this time a tad more urgently, "Lake ahead!!!"

This time I was going faster, having gotten more comfortable with all the windy, rolling, narrow roads. I had to slam on my breaks even harder this time. After our van careened to a stop, we took a moment to look at the same water we had greeted face-to-face just days before. This time we were on a more intimate basis. After a moment of stunned silence and disbelief, we looked at each other, and this time we could barely catch our breaths from the laughter that rolled forth from the shock. Again?! Really?!... *At this point, I should have started singing, "Julie, take the wheel" Carrie Underwood style.*

Because it ended well, taking wrong roads was really funny. And we still talk about it to this day. But usually taking wrong roads is frustrating and time-consuming. It keeps us from going where we need to be.

Life roads are the same.

If we're not paying attention, we can choose the wrong road. Sometimes we find ourselves off course by accident. Other times we are distracted. Then there are times when we choose the wrong road stubbornly, ignoring all the warning signs posted along the way. It only takes one wrong turn to get us—and sometimes even our loved ones—in a heap of trouble.

Turning around can be tricky too. Mistakes like that can't always be undone easily. They may take a bit of time winding our way back to the right road again. Fortunately, God is always there encouraging us along.

Listening to God's Word, Holy Spirit, and wise friends keeps us from going down the wrong road. Their voices cry out loud warnings to us of the dangerously cold water or dense foliage ahead.

The question is, "Will we listen?"

Turn your ear to wisdom and apply your heart to understanding. For the Lord gives wisdom, and from his mouth come knowledge and understanding. For he guards the course of the just and protects the way of his faithful ones. Then you will understand

what is right and just and fair—every good path.
—Proverbs 2:2, 6, 8-9

The way of fools seems right to them, but the wise listen to advice.
—Proverbs 12:15

But the Advocate, the Holy Spirit, whom the Father will send in my name, will teach you all things and will remind you of everything I have said to you.
—John 14:26

When should I have listened to my friends? Is there a situation now where I need to listen to the guidance of the Holy Spirit?

It is Decidedly So

Jo

Honesty is the first chapter in the book of wisdom.
—Thomas Jefferson

I was rummaging around in the chest where I keep my childhood belongings when I came across a well-worn toy from my youth—The Magic 8 Ball. Maybe you had one too? Perhaps, like me and my grade-school friends, you used to ask this magic ball if a certain boy in your math class might someday ask you out on a date, and then squealed with delight when the fortune-telling ball revealed, "It is decidedly so."

Perhaps your questions were a bit more mature in nature like: "Will I go to college? Will I get married? Should I say 'Yes' to that job opportunity?" Chances are, that Magic 8 Ball didn't always get it right, and your reliance on such toys faded soon enough along with acid-washed jeans and Bonnie Bell lip gloss. I, too, found the same flaws in the ball's ability to direct me down the right path. That's how my Magic 8 Ball found its way to the bottom of my chest.

I hadn't lost the desire to gain direction and advice; I just figured the Magic 8 Ball might not be the way for me to get it.

So how does a person gain the ability to make right choices? I've noticed that a series of right business decisions can land a person that job they've always wanted. A couple of right decisions can heal a strained relationship or bring restoration to a difficult situation. In the same way, the choice to spew hate can cause relationships to end, and a couple of bad career choices can land you in the unemployment line.

When the Lord asked Solomon what he wanted from God, Solomon could have chosen riches or fame or the power to kill his enemies. He could have chosen to have the most beautiful woman on earth or the largest kingdom ever known. But instead, Solomon asked God for *wisdom* (1 Kings 3:12), and God granted him a wise and discerning heart.

> *"So, give your servant a discerning heart to govern your people and to distinguish between right and wrong. For who is able to govern this great people of yours?"*
>
> *The Lord was pleased that Solomon had asked for this. So, God said to him, "Since you have asked for this and not for long life or wealth for yourself, nor have asked for the death of your enemies but for discernment in administering justice, I will do what you have asked.*
>
> *I will give you a wise and discerning heart, so that there will never have been anyone like you, nor will there ever be.*
> —1 Kings 3:9-12

Thankfully, Solomon shared many of his wise sayings with us in the book of Proverbs.

This book of short truths tells us that people who have wisdom enjoy its benefits. The person who has wisdom, for example, is faithful and trusts in the Lord. The wise put God first and turn away from evil. The wise know right from wrong; they listen and learn. Wise people do what is right.

But Solomon isn't the only person to receive wisdom. God is generous with his gifts of discernment. James writes, "If any of you lacks wisdom, you should ask God, who gives generously to all without finding fault, and it will be given to you" (James 1:5). This wisdom isn't something we have to chase after or save money to purchase. Wisdom isn't a resource a psychic can sell or a secret a horoscope can reveal. In fact, consulting these sources would likely be considered *unwise*. Rather, wisdom is something that we receive by drawing near to God and asking for it.

So, I'll put my Magic 8 Ball back in its spot at the bottom of my chest. I'll remember fondly the wonder and excitement of childhood superstitions. But to receive true wisdom and guidance and advice for my life, I'll turn my eyes back to the Word of God. And I'll remember the words of wise King Solomon:

> *Trust in the Lord with all your heart, and lean*
> *not on your own understanding. In all your*
> *ways acknowledge him and he will*
> *direct your path.*
> —Proverbs 3:5-6

Where in my life do I need to seek God's wisdom?

Untied Shoe Laces

LuAnn

Lessons in life will be repeated until they are learned.
—Frank Sonnenberg

The wise old owl sat on an oak,
The more he saw, the less he spoke,
The less he spoke, the more he heard,
Why aren't we like that wise old bird?
—Charles M. Schulz

"Hold up! Stop!" I yelled.

The little boy with the mop of brown hair stopped suddenly on the playground, looking at me wide-eyed. I'm sure he thought by my reaction that a space creature had landed nearby or that he had done something terribly wrong.

I ran over, stooped down, started tying his shoe laces, and started in on my sermon. "Do you know how dangerous it is to run with your shoe untied? That makes me so nervous! You could trip and hurt yourself... Okay, now you can run and play!"

And he was off to bigger and better things, eager to escape the crazy shoelace guardian.

Although watching kids tear around on the playground each day brought me great joy, I was a stickler as a grade school playground monitor on kids having their shoes tied, among other safety virtues.

Fast forward to this past November.

I had been helping at a retreat all day and thought upon my return it was a good idea to get my dogs' energy out by taking them on a quick run before dark. Soon after, our threesome ran into a couple that was moving at sloth speed along with their two bull dogs. They were not an older couple, and I couldn't quite figure out why they kept stopping and why they were moving so slowly. Finally, my impatience got the best of me as I was tired of reining my dogs back from their desire to introduce themselves to this pokey entourage.

I thought, "I'll just run on the left side of the street for a ways and then cut back to the sidewalk once I'm far enough ahead of them." I passed them in no time at all. I saw a car coming down the street towards me so I upped my sprint as I cut back to the sidewalk.

But, I didn't make it.

The next thing I knew my chin was bouncing off the cement, and I felt things rearrange in my head. It took me a minute to realize what had happened as I lay splayed out upon the paved road in shock.

Once I started to get my bearings, embarrassment took over. I got up only to quickly realized my left knee had taken the major blow and didn't want to hold my weight. But, I wasn't seeing stars like I thought I would, and that encouraged me.

I looked back to see what was going on with the car that had been coming towards me, but it was nowhere to be seen.

Then I looked down to see my long, dark grey shoe laces. "Really?!" I thought. "I'm in pain because I tripped on my untied shoe laces?" I always double tied those long round laces that easily came undone. But in my haste, not this day.

A part of me realized I was quite injured, but for some reason, I kept walking—or rather limping—the dogs. Once I got to the woods and lake, one of my dogs, Daisy, wouldn't leave me to take her run, which should have been another clue. I was hurting all over pretty badly so I finally had the idea of taking my camera out and putting it in selfie mode—a rarity for us older folks—to assess the damage. I was shocked when my reflection sported blood all over my face, vest, white shirt, and coat. And my chin was growing an extra bump. "Lovely," I thought. I limped home with ever-increasing pain in my left leg.

When I got home, I put my bloody clothes in the wash, taped an ice pack around my knee, washed and sterilized my face, held paper towels to my chin for a while and then put huge band-aids on it that I had to frequently change and continued to hobble around unpacking from the retreat and doing other work.

When my husband got home, he was not happy that I was not icing my knee and sitting with my leg raised. By morning my left knee was swollen like a grapefruit; I could put no weight on my leg.

My husband found some crutches for me from some bike racing friends of ours—well-familiar with sport injuries—and Doug was kind enough to run them over.

I didn't go in to the doctor, despite many friends' encouragement. So, several days later a dear friend ended up rushing me to the ER. My brain felt like it was on fire (effects I was to learn later of not properly taking care of a concussion).

Seven weeks later, my left knee still hurt and I had a scar on my chin.

Foolishness. On very many fronts.

And as bad as my consequences were for my foolishness in this situation, some unwise choices and consequences can be, and have been, even more devastating.

The book of Proverbs has a lot to say about foolishness. Thankfully, it also gives us a picture of what wisdom looks like as well. In fact, foolishness and wisdom are what most of this little book in the Bible deals with.

The NIV Mom's Devotional Bible describes Proverbs as a book that "offers practical wisdom drawn from experiences common to all people and expresses that wisdom in brief, pithy sayings…and clearly shows the different outcomes for those who follow God's wisdom and for those who do not." Dictionary.com describes proverbs as "Containing the sayings of sages; a wise or profound saying or precept."

Let's take a look at some of the descriptions used in this book to describe the foolish:

- Despises, resents or ignores wisdom, discipline, knowledge, advise, and correction.

- Is a mocker *(treat with ridicule or contempt; mimic derisively; deceive).*

- Delights in doing wrong and rejoices in evil.

- Does not know what makes her stumble *(untied shoelaces).*

- Does not obey teachers or listen to instructors.

- Lacks discipline.

- Is led astray by folly *(an unwise undertaking; foolishness).*

- Repeats her foolishness.

- Conceals sin.

- Malicious *(intentionally harmful; spiteful).*

- Is prideful and haughty.

- Shows no discretion.

- Pretends to be someone she is not.

- Chases fantasies.

- Thinks her ways are right.

- Shows annoyance easily.

- Answers before listening.

- Stirs up dissention.

- Hangs around fools.

- Does not seek counsel.

Now let's look at how Solomon, the main writer, describes the wise in contrast.

- Trusts in the Lord.

- Does not give in to sinner's enticements; shuns evil.

- Delights in, calls out to, and seeks wisdom and knowledge more than gold or silver; values wisdom and knowledge more than rubies.

- Leans not on her own understanding and is not wise in her own eyes.

- Acknowledges God, commits her plans to the Lord and seeks his guidance.

- Honors the Lord with her wealth.

- Does not despise the Lord's discipline; understands it is because he loves her.

- Is discerning.

- Gives generously.

- Does not falsely accuse.

- Does not envy.

- Guards her heart.

- Avoids adultery and anything that could lead up to it at all costs.

- Practices discretion.

- Practices sound judgment; is just and fair.

- Rebukes, instructs, and teaches the wise and righteous.

- Is diligent and not lazy.

- Covers wrongs and overlooks offenses and insults.

- Has many advisers and listens to advice.

- Speech is known for being: wise, healing, nourishing, honest, kind, pleasant, and the right thing to say and when to say it. She knows when to not say anything and is not a gossip.

- Shows humility.

- Guided by integrity.

- Produces fruit that wins souls.

- Promotes peace.

- Is cautious in friendship; walks with the wise and stays away from foolish and hot-tempered people.

- Is a light that shines brightly.

- Cares about justice for the poor and needy and speaks up for them. Is kind to the needy and feeds them.

I think it is wise to learn from Solomon, considered to be one of the wisest men to ever live. Let us take some time to humble our hearts and look over both lists. Let the Spirit talk to us.

Although Christ's blood has made us pure in God's sight, we still walk in the flesh and in foolishness at times. And doing so has very negative consequences. Let's identify those areas of wisdom we want to add, as well as any areas of even a shadow of foolishness we may hold, and turn them over to Christ's cleansing work.

Our heavenly father, thank you for guiding us and helping us understand what wisdom looks like, as you are the source of all wisdom. And as the Proverbs say, wisdom was around before even the earth was formed and was with you as you formed the earth and everything in it. Help us to value and seek wisdom more than any earthly possession.

What areas in my life do I need to operate from a place of wisdom instead of foolishness?

Discovering Faith

When the Sun Stood Still

Heidi

If we have the audacity to ask, God has the ability to perform.

—Steve Furtick

Ever since my first-born was just a tiny kicking blob on an ultrasound, I've debated about his life verse. There's so many compelling nuggets in Scripture that could ennoble him to live a faith-filled life…but I was always stuck on the cliché, oh-so-common verse in Joshua: "This is my command—be strong and courageous! Do not be afraid or discouraged. For the Lord your God is with you wherever you go" (1:9).

Shouldn't I be more creative though? This verse was announced at my college graduation ceremony, screen-printed on the back of my volleyball warm-up tee, etched into half of the mugs in my cupboard, and at the risk of sounding melodramatic, it's splashed across every other Christian trinket you could possibly find around the globe.

But. Even so. I'm convicted with the thought that its over-use shouldn't diminish the potency of what this verse delivers. Because there's power among these words. So much strength to draw from. And it introduces a character in the Bible with such sure faith—exactly what I hope for in my son.

So yes, I'm stuck on that man Joshua. The one with the audacious faith that made the sun stand still. And I'm talking literally. Joshua needed more time to defeat his enemies, but in order to do that, he needed daylight. So, when evening hours hit and the sun started to dip down, Joshua very simply asked God to pause it from falling further. To freeze time for his people. Who would even think to pray that prayer? To believe that God will literally stop the world for him? Stop the scientific order that faithfully repeats itself like clockwork day-in and day-out? Joshua. And God gave him exactly what he asked for.

Joshua was also the one that God chose to lead the Israelites into the promised land. Before they could get there though, they found themselves shaking in their boots facing a barred-up city with intimidating walls as high as they could see. How could they get around? God didn't send flaming arrows to Joshua's aide, nor an earthquake to crumble the obstacle down. Instead, he told Joshua to silently walk around the walls six times in six days. And on the seventh, he'd see a miracle. And guess what? He did.

So, Joshua 1:9 has been chosen for my now sweet toddler.

And as I come across this verse (inevitably) at a Christian event, sermon, or bookstore, I'm reminded of this prayer for my son. And the wheels keep spinning, and I keep thinking, what if we all made Joshua 1:9 our life verse? What if those who call themselves believers also make this verse their focal point? The heartbeat of their faith? The command that echoes deep within our core?

What would this world look like if we all lived out of a faith just as audacious as this man Joshua? That we would ask Jesus for our own suns to stand still? That we would know just how ready he is to act for us if we would just be bold enough to ask, not just for a good morning or a better tomorrow, but for the impossible?

That when the walls of life seem impossibly high and insurmountable, we wouldn't give up hoping and stop on day six? But rather, hold strong to God's character and see his miracles through. As the walls crash around us and we stand tall praising God among the ruins of our challenges, then, just maybe, we would bear witness to the One who never disappoints, and the world couldn't help but take notice.

As I watch my toddler play and dream dreams for his future, I truly believe he is here to make a sun-stand-still-size difference, and if I have big dreams for him, I can't imagine the puffy, grandeur plans our God has for our lives too. As his people, let's be strong and courageous enough to find out. Instead of giving in to fear or discouragement, let's instead ask the Lord for the unthinkable. And let's be the Joshua's of our day, moving forward in the confidence that God is with us wherever we go— when we do, be ready to see the sun stand still in our lives today.

Where may God be calling me to set fear aside and replace it with his strength and courage?

No More Excuses

Jo

*Your hardest times often lead to the greatest
moments of your life. Keep going.*
—Roy T. Bennett

What do you think a person's life looks like when he or she
actually lives *by faith*? Would a life lived *by faith* mean that
someone was not affected by fear, or complaint, or that little
voice that whispers, *I can't.*

Hebrews 11 highlights story after story of biblical heroes who
accomplished much *by faith*. One of those heroes is Moses.
Moses is credited for surviving a murderous plot on his life,
escaping Pharaoh's command, leading his people out of Egypt,
crossing the Red Sea, and leading his people to the Promised
Land. Before he started his journey, Moses even saw and heard
the Lord speak to him from a burning bush, directing him to go.

Now most of us would like to think that if we saw and heard
from God, up close like Moses did, nothing could stop us from
fulfilling his call on our lives. But Moses still wasn't so sure.

We pick up his story in Exodus, chapter 3.

> *Then the Lord told him, "I have certainly seen the
> oppression of my people in Egypt. I have heard their cries
> of distress because of their harsh slave drivers. Yes, I am
> aware of their suffering. So, I have come down to rescue
> them from the power of the Egyptians and lead them out of
> Egypt into their own fertile and spacious land. It is a land
> flowing with milk and honey. Look! The cry of the people*

of Israel has reached me, and I have seen how harshly the Egyptians abuse them. Now go, for I am sending you to Pharaoh. You must lead my people out of Egypt."
(vs. 7-10)

Now at this point, you can just imagine Moses looking around—hoping that God was talking to someone else. After all, Moses was hiding out in the desert because he'd killed a man. He'd been running from everyone…including God. So, he asks, "Who am I to appear before Pharaoh? Who am I to lead people out of Egypt?" (Exodus 3:11)

God could have reasoned with Moses about how his experience in Pharaoh's household prepared him for this job. He could have revealed the gifts and talents that Moses possessed but just didn't know about yet. But instead, God offers a simple promise to Moses. He simply says, "But I will be with you." (Exodus 3:12a)

But for Moses, that was not enough. He continues to make excuses.

I'm not trustworthy.

I'm not credible.

I'm not qualified.

Moses had an identity problem. He knew himself a little too well. He knew his past. He knew his failures. He knew his deficits. We seem to be very good at knowing our faults, our past, and our deficits too. I know I've had that same identity crisis. I've given those same excuses. I've tried to bargain with, reason with, and hide from God. You see, while it sounds good…this living *by faith* is difficult. I like to know the end game. I like to see what's behind the curtain. I like to see the finish line before I run the race.

Maybe you've had to battle the same type of identity problem when God has asked you to step out *by faith*. Who am I to parent a teenager? Who am I to take that job? Who am I to go back to school, to teach that course, to lead that discussion group? Maybe that question is going through your head today because you've been asked to step out of your comfort zone. It happens to me often, and I always seem to come up with the same excuses.

Moses knew his deficits too, and he was reaching out for something, for anything to save him from having to do the inevitable. He was afraid to *take the first step.* In order for God to work in your life and mine, we need to take the first step.

When Moses listed his excuses, our merciful and loving God countered each one with a promise of his own. God lists his promises one by one.

You may not be anyone special but *I AM*, and I will go with you.

Your name may not be trustworthy but *MINE IS*, and you can use it.

You may not be credible on your own but *I AM*, and you will operate under my strength.

You say you're not qualified but *I QUALIFY YOU*, and that's all the prerequisite that you need.

Where do you feel weak? Where do you feel inadequate? In what situation do you feel absolutely hopeless? When is it that you want to say to God, *please...find someone else!*

I'm going to suggest that it is when you feel at your weakest, when you feel most inadequate, that it is at that point when God may be asking you to go, to take a step, to walk *by faith*. He may be asking you to get up and walk, even though you don't know the terrain, even though you don't know what lies behind the curtain, even though you can't see the finish line. Take a step. And trust that he is with you, that he will equip you, and that he will give you the power you need once you take the first step.

May we—like Moses—trust that when God calls us to a task, he will equip us with what we need to see it through. May we—like Moses—have the courage to take the first step *by faith*.

As I was with Moses, so I will be with you; I will never leave you
nor forsake you.
—Joshua 1:5

In what area in my life do I need to step out in faith?

When God Says Wait

Julie

I talk to God but the sky is empty.
—Sylvia Plath

Sometimes life just doesn't make sense.

Like when you finally reach a stage in life when you and your spouse can fly the coop and enjoy time just the two of you...then divorce papers are filed, or an illness strikes or you are left alone at a graveside without a chance to say goodbye.

Or when the child you have loved and nurtured turns against you, or turns to alcohol or drugs, or disappears without a trace.

Recently I've been talking to God about my second-born son. He has been struggling, too, but, not with anger or alcohol issues. He is my high achiever. He graduated from his college and master's degree programs with a 4.0. He is incredibly diligent, meticulous, and detail-oriented, and if given a chance, would make a phenomenal employee. But, for two years he has struggled to land a job in his field. He has worked as a janitor, in an amp shop and with a professor to make ends meet.

After two years of beseeching the heavens, I told my hubby the other day that I feel as if my prayers have been bouncing off the ceiling.

And I know that I'm not the only one to question where God is when our cries for help go unanswered. I'm not the only one who wonders why he leaves us lingering so long.

After reading Luke 7:19-20 recently, I got the sense that was exactly how John the Baptist felt when he found himself languishing behind prison bars. And who could blame him? He was, after all, the prophetic *"voice calling in the wilderness,"* that Isaiah, long years back, had talked about (40:3). And now, he had no voice at all. As days passed into weeks, then into months, then into a year or more, he began to question. Question his calling. Question if he'd heard God right. Question if Jesus was...well, read it for yourself, *"Are you the one we heard was coming, or should we wait for someone else?"*

When life's difficulties seem to drag on and on, it can do a number on us. Our minds whirl, our stomachs churn, our bodies toss restless in our beds. And when our prayers seem to go unanswered, we question. We question God's goodness. Question his ability to work on our behalf. Question whether we should be looking elsewhere for answers.

I brought this burden of mine for my son to my spiritual director. She is a beautiful, gentle woman of faith. I am forever grateful to God for her guidance.

She asked me to close my eyes and imagine myself smack dab in the middle of this seemingly impossible situation. After some time in silence she queried, *"Where is God in the midst of these things?"*

To be honest, I couldn't find him anywhere.

But, then a memory sprang to mind—a memory of my firstborn son, Erik, who was then four or five. He had pulled our wedding album out and was perusing it on the sofa. I decided to sit down beside him and look through it with him. When we got to the end, he had a strange look on his face.

He then opened the album back up again, this time scouring the pages feverishly. Not finding what he was looking for he asked, *"Mom, why am I not in any of these pictures?"* I chuckled and said, *"Hon, you weren't in the pictures because you weren't born yet."* He looked at me very seriously and said, *"Oh yes I was! I was in the balcony; you just didn't see me!"*

Those words...*Oh yes, I was! I was in the balcony; you just didn't see me*...echoed in my heart.

That was it! That is where God is. Not in an actual balcony, of course, but, he is there...even when we cannot see him, even when there hasn't been an answer to our prayers in some time. God not only hears them, he is smack dab in the middle of all those circumstances. And that speaks peace into my soul while I wait.

> *If Christ spent an anguished night in prayer, if He burst out from the Cross, 'My God, my God, why have you forsaken me?' then surely, we are also permitted doubt. But we must move on. To choose doubt as a philosophy of life is akin to choosing immobility as a means of transportation.*
> —Yann Martel

> *At just the right time, I will respond to you.*
> —Isaiah 49:8a

> *In time, you will see*
> *that the greatest of gifts is to truly know me.*
> *And though oft my answers seem terribly late,*
> *my most precious answer of all is still... "Wait."*
> —Russell Kelfer

What area in my life do I need to wait "just a little longer?"

Sometimes It Gets Messy Before It Gets Good

Heidi

Beginnings are always messy.
—John Galsworthy

Last year, our family moved into a charming, full-of-character, little blue house that was built in the 1920's.

Almost everything is beautiful in its own regard: The wide farmhouse sink. The French doors peeking into the living room. The sturdy hardwood floors. The composed clawfoot tub in the upstairs bathroom. And since we are in no way Chip and Joanna Gaines, my husband and I breathed a deep sigh of relief when the inspection came back clear, and it was move-in ready! Nothing to fix, change, or update.

Well, *almost* nothing.

When you walk into our kitchen, sure, you first see the woodworking of our tall cabinets paired with that drool-worthy farmhouse sink. (To which my husband *actually* said, "We will take this out, right?" I can almost hear you gasping through the pages. I know, readers...I have since enlightened him.)

But when you look to the left, you see a randomly placed stove and when you look to the right you see a floating fridge, and when you take a closer look, you see no countertop space, and I hate to even write this down, but *no dishwasher*. It's random. And ugly. And somewhat maddening.

So, this week, we've looked our kitchen square in the eye and started making progress towards renovating it into something functional and aligning the charm with rest of the house. Starting with the paint.

We (and I mean we, as in my husband) laid down the prime the other night, and as I walked into the kitchen to see the progress as only a dutiful contractor would, he quickly said, "It's just the prime! There's streaks and you can still see the wood paneling underneath, but don't panic. It's going to take a few coats to get it to look how we imagined." *He knew* I would panic. Lift my eyebrows. And wonder what we were thinking trying to DIY. *He knew* I would be skeptical, discouraged by what appeared a messy situation. Because I like to see betterment in the progress.

But sometimes, it gets messy before it gets good. Have you ever experienced that?

Your marriage is falling apart, but before you can reconcile any differences, it may take a counselor to unravel and discover deeper where things went wrong in the first place.

Or maybe you were let go from your job and ended up taking a salary cut and a less-amazing benefit package with your new position; but years later, you realized the promotions and fulfillment you gained at this new role could never have happened at your previous company, and you find yourself incredibly grateful.

Or maybe you were diagnosed with cancer and went through countless rounds of chemotherapy. It seemed messy and chaotic and scary in the thick of things, but you made it into remission and now you're actually exercising and eating well and relating to others in ways you never did before.

We may not see that today. We may not even want to see tomorrow. We may be panicking about our circumstances today, our progress today, our job, our marriage, our kids, our weight, our success today. But we were never meant to do it alone. This is when we lean on others that *can* see the light at the end of the tunnel, or the growth and improvement we've had along the way. This is when we surround ourselves and confide in people who say, "Don't panic! Take heart! Jesus has already overcome."

For me and my kitchen walls, that was my husband—and he was right. The next day and another coat later, my walls were brighter and smoother. I can actually picture how it's going to look in the end, and I'm getting excited.

And it just tells me, that sometimes, we have to push through to another day. We may be in the dark hour, the valley, and things may look crummy and disheartening. But our God tells us to always be a people of hope, because he is *always* working. He is *always* by our side. And He promises to work *all things* for our good. Whatever your lot may be, he indeed is turning the table towards your favor—we can be sure of that, brothers and sisters of Christ.

How may God be working in an area of my life that appears messy and discouraging?

Defeating the Wall

Jo

Faith is, picture it done.
–Josiah Cullen

My kids are obsessed with the show, *American Ninja Warrior*. It is a program of intense moments, showing men and women tackling an obstacle course of tremendously difficult challenges, starting with the easier feats and moving on to these crazy, complicated tests of physical endurance. One of the most difficult obstacles is the "warped wall." It's a nearly vertical climb of 12 feet…that means these people are basically running up a wall in Spiderman fashion, without a web to assist them.

One of the women who completed the course was asked how she tackled the warped wall obstacle. She said, "I picture myself getting *over* the wall, not getting *up* the wall."

I only wish I could apply that kind of philosophy to the walls I face. Whether it's a physical hurdle, a relational wall, or a spiritual one, I tend to stand at the bottom and stare at the problem—wondering how I'm ever going to make it *up*.

I have a little plaque on my front hall table that says, "Faith is… picture it done," a quote penned by Josiah Cullen, an 11-year-old boy who has an innate gift to see God's words in action.

So why does it seem that when faced with an obstacle, we tend to focus on the obstacle itself, instead on the power of the One who can not only get us *over* the wall—but can even *destroy* it if he chooses?

The Israelites faced a similar battle of the mind when Joshua led them to the walled city of Jericho. God had given specific instructions on how that wall was to come down. The Israelites were to surround Jericho, but not in the traditional fashion. In ancient times, armies would plan a surprise attack either late at night or early in the morning. No, this group of Israelites was to simply walk around the city in plain sight seven times and then blow their trumpets and yell. Then, the wall would come down.

Really?

I can imagine this group of non-soldiers walking around the city, looking up at that wall, trying to devise a plan on how they might spot a crack in the wall that they could muscle through. They had to be thinking about a backup plan for what would happen if God did not come through with what he said he would do.

Because sometimes his plans seem a little bit strange. Sometimes his plans don't make a lot of sense. Sometimes, *most times*, his plans are a bit unconventional. It's almost like God is saying, "Will you trust me?"

Jesus says I must love my enemies…even those who despise me.

I say, *Really?*

He says, *Will you trust me?*

Jesus says I must forgive the person who has wronged me, not just once but *every* time.

I say, *Really?*

He says, *Will you trust me?*

God says walk around that wall, and I will tear it down for you.

I say, *Really?*

He says, *Will you trust me?*

Proverbs 3:4 says, *Trust in the Lord with all your heart. Lean not on your own understanding.*

Whatever impossible situation we're facing, we tend to want to figure out a plan, get things done, get ourselves out of it, but God says, *Wait...Listen.* I know you think you have a plan of how this is all going to work out, but Trust *Me.* Trust in *My* plan, lean not in your own understanding.

Will you trust Me?

And as we look at this story, the culmination of a 40-year journey through the desert, and we read about this crazy plan, and even crazier still that this army of Israelites followed it, and we read that after the seventh lap on the seventh day with the people shouting and the horns blasting that the wall came crumbling down, we can only come to one conclusion...God gets the glory. Because when the problem is tall, when the plan is unconventional, and when victory comes, it can only be God who gets the glory.

So, I will try to change my perspective. Instead of being overwhelmed by the size of my wall, I will be overwhelmed by the strength and wisdom of my God. For when he ushers in a plan or vision that seems a bit unconventional, I know that he is making way for a glorious victory, one that can only be claimed by him.

And that means my only job is to picture it *done.*

We have to pray with our eyes on God, not on the difficulties.
–Oswald Chambers

Where in my life do I need to "picture it done?"

Discovering How to Let Go

Burdensome Baggage

Julie

*Your journey will be much easier and lighter if you don't carry
your past with you.*
—Unknown

Carrying any baggage around with you? Oh…I'm not talking
about those extra pounds we all put on over the holidays. Or
even the balance pending on your credit cards. What I'm talking
about is the emotional stuff we lug around with us—old junk that
we just can't seem to shake off—excess luggage like old
grudges, hurt feelings, discouragement, nagging worries and
cares.

I sure feel like I am carrying a big old suitcase or two with me
this year.

The problem with carrying that burdensome stuff around with us
is that it doesn't just weigh on your mind, it weighs down your
heart and impacts your life.

It leaves you wide-eyed at night. It shadows you during the day.
You try to release it. You beg God to take it. But, somehow it
still haunts you.

Over the last few weeks I've been reading through the book of
Proverbs. When I came to chapter nine, the following verse
jumped right out at me. It stopped me in my tracks:

> *Leave your old ways behind and live!*
> *—Proverbs 9:6*

Why is it so hard to leave those old ways behind? Why do we struggle so with carrying these burdens from one year to the next?

I think one reason is that after a spell, we grow accustomed to them. Oh, we don't like insomnia any more than the next person, but, there is also something oddly comforting in bearing old grudges, in feeling justified in hanging on to hurts others have inflicted. And, how can one not feel a bit discouraged these days when we look around at the chaos in our world? Or if you're one for whom the floor fell out of your life or out of the life of a loved one, how can you not carry that around with you everywhere you go?

I've tried the directive that Peter gave to us to "Cast all of our anxiety on Jesus because he cares for us." (1ˢᵗ Peter 5:7). But, my problem with casting them away is that my upper body strength and my will are pretty wimpy. I have tried giving these bags of mine the heave ho, but, they don't get very far. Seeing them just feet in front of me, I find it easier just to go pick them up again.

No, I find that leaving them behind once and for all is much more difficult than I had anticipated.

As is the way that God often works when he starts stirring deep in the heart of you, the same story line appears again and again in your life. Like this devotional I opened to one morning...

> *Bury every fear of the future, of poverty for those dear to you, of suffering, of loss. Bury all thought of unkindness and bitterness, all your dislikes, your resentments, your sense of failure, your disappointment in others and in yourself, your gloom, your despondency, and leave them all, buried, and go forward to a new and risen life.*
> —A.J. Russell

There it was again. In order to leave that lumber-some luggage of the past behind—I have to bury it. Burying it…leaving it behind…leads to life. It was all coming together for me.

But, then, to really drive the point home, God caught my attention while I was out and about one afternoon running errands. Turning the radio on, I heard this song by Nichole Nordeman, and I knew what God wanted me to do. He wanted me to bury those things I carried once and for all in the baptismal waters of his love.

Sunlit shoreline
Where I was baptized
This time dark skies
Leave me capsized

Some storms claim you
Some will rename you
My hands reach high
Be my lifeline

This is the river where I went under
This is the river where I come up new

Oh God, be my rescue
Oh God, be my rescue
And save me from myself
Save me from myself

Oh God be my rescue tonight

Watching the old me
Slowly sinking
Hope is rising up
I can feel the rush
I'm alive and I'm breathing

This is the river where I go under
This is the river where I come up new

Baptized in the blood and wonder
This is the river that I fall into
When I fall into You

Just like baptismal waters. I myself had to go under, baggage and all, watching the old me, the burdened me, slowly sinking out of sight and feel hope rise up, feel the rush of air fill my lungs as I came up new.

Leaving behind what we've carried too long is the only way to *live*.

> *I am the resurrection and the life.*
> —John 11:25

What is God calling me to let go of?

Expectations

Heidi

Being confident of this, that he who began a good work in you
will carry it on to completion until the day of Christ Jesus.
—Philippians 1:6

I used to click my heels into my college classes, smooth out my pencil skirt with matching blouse, and confidently stand before my classmates for presentations on market share, conversion rates, and customer acquisition costs. This was all so energizing as a marketing major, and I envisioned myself down the road bustling around a quick-paced advertising agency, becoming a successful project manager of sorts, and quickly climbing the corporate ladder to utter greatness. Dream big, right?

But after exploring internships and experiencing work cultures, I realized so much of the for-profit world was cut-throat and bottom-line driven. Bulldozing you as a person, all for the sake of earning revenue and keeping stockholders happy. And I just wasn't into that.

So, I went into ministry. Where I taught hundreds of kids Bible stories, pumped up a volunteer base in the mission to serve Christ, and even grabbed a spot behind our church's podium because I was told I was compelling with my words and inspiring with my vision.

And I felt that. I felt energy brimming over inside of me, and I knew I was working in my element. Fulfilled beyond measure, I saw myself powerfully being used by Christ, and blessed to call it all work.

But there was a stronger call within me. I had just gotten married to the most wonderful man in the world, and we couldn't wait to start a family. So, we didn't! Ten months later, we welcomed our sweet boy, Oscar Tyler, into the world—and the moment I saw him, I cried enough happy tears to fill the Pacific Ocean, and I soon gave my two weeks' notice.

My expectations? They were Pinterest-board worthy. I would wake up every morning to a snuggly baby who would patiently wait for his milk. Breastfeed effortlessly. Cart around said flexible baby with the car seat easily hooked in my arm. Take long, relaxing walks around the neighborhood. Have hours of me-time while baby naps. And schedule loads of coffee dates to catch up with friends.

But I soon came to find that motherhood looked different. Actually, *quite* different.

My baby N-E-V-E-R wanted to snuggle; he was so independent right out of the gate. He also wasn't patient when it came time to warm up his milk; he would scream, turn beat red, and cry crocodile tears even if it was just 30 quick seconds of waiting. Breastfeeding was a challenge too, and after three tough months, I resigned to pumping exclusively.

And the CAR SEAT. SO HEAVY. I don't know how other moms look so effortless with theirs coolly resting in the crook of the arm, because I was sweating bullets when I simply lugged that thing from the garage into the house. And sometimes, the walks around the neighborhood were nice, but sometimes, the crisp air was filled with the cries of my baby instead, and it seemed like whenever we did get out, we had to rush back in for the next feeding anyway.

And those naps? No energy left to read, clean, or even scroll through my once-beloved Pinterest boards; rather, I crashed on the couch every spare minute I could find. And catching up with friends? Who can actually finish a complete conversation (let alone a complete sentence!) when your baby is like a magnet to every breakable insight?

My problem was I assumed I'd feel the same way in motherhood as I did in college and in ministry—made for it. Confident in my choices. Compelling in my directions. Respected in my leadership. Energized all day. And always feeling affirmed every step of the way.

But it's not like your baby praises you, "Great job, mom!" when you successfully put them down for a nap, and your toddler doesn't always listen when you tell him to eat his vegetables or stop screaming in the aisles at Target. And you may not feel powerfully used by God when you're wiping floors and butts all day either.

However, here's the truth—for every mom and every Christ-follower alike. Not every calling is easy and manageable and undemanding. We do have an enemy on the loose, and sin does intersect with our world every day. But even amidst the trouble or challenge we face, when God gives us a calling, he will surely see it through.

Moses didn't feel confident enough to confront Pharaoh, and Gideon thought himself under-resourced to save God's people from the Midianites. Queen Esther felt out of place, and Jeremiah doubted he had all the answers. And even in their lacking, nothing could thwart God's plans—no obstacle, giant, or mountain, no element of fear, no feeling of despair, being less than, or ill-equipped.

Through his power, Moses freed the Israelites from slavery, Gideon led God's people into victory, Esther risked her life to save the Jews—and through her bravery, they were spared—and Jeremiah was powerfully used as God's chosen prophet to speak truth to his people.

The truth is still the truth today. God has called us to be mothers, fathers, teachers, mentors, coaches, artists, and businessmen and women.

We may feel inadequate, and our path may not be ridden with rainbows, butterflies and unicorns at every turn. But God does not call us without empowering us. And with his ever-powerful presence always surrounding us and helping us, we really have no reason to think otherwise. We must claim the truth that "the Lord *will* fulfill his purpose for me" (Psalm 138:8).

Whatever that looks like for you, take heart in knowing that God is with you, has equipped you, and will help you. He will surely see you through. Choose today to let your weakness and insecurities be a platform of God's power, and "may he equip you with all you need for doing his will. May he produce in you, through the power of Jesus Christ, every good thing that is pleasing to him. All glory to him forever and ever! Amen." (Hebrews 13:21)

What area in my life do I feel most inadequate, and how has God equipped me for this role already?

God's Divine Paintbrush

Julie

A canvas: linen, muslin, sometimes a panel; then the gesso—a primary coat, always white. A layer of underpaint, usually a pastel color, then, the miracle, where the secrets are: the paint itself, swished around, roughly, gently, layer on layer, thick or thin, not more than a quarter of an inch ever—God can happen in that quarter of an inch.
—Steve Martin

I first caught a glimpse of him out of the corner of my eye.

As I panned across the conservatory's colorfully riotous display of flowers, I spied a bent-over elderly figure, seated on a bench, tucked between the lilies and cyclamen.

There he was quietly working. His paints, brushes, water jars and a completed canvas lay spread out beside him.

I was drawn to him like a moth to flame.

I tucked myself into a little nook, just behind him, where I could watch as he delicately worked his craft. His first strokes were a watercolor wash of teal blue-green. When his backdrop was dry, he took out a pencil and lightly drew the outline of the flower he intended to paint. He dipped his fine brush into the water jar, then into red paint, then added white and worked them together to get just the right shade of pink.

Each sweep of his brush had intention. Each swirl. Each stroke. He knew what he wanted to accomplish. One-flower-at-a-time.

To my untrained eye, however, there were times when he'd add a color that looked muddied or seemed to ruin the work altogether. But, a line of paint would be added, giving definition. And before I knew it, what I thought to be a mistake, transformed into a thing of beauty.

Isn't that the way God works his brush strokes across the canvas of our lives?

He, too, like my elderly friend, goes about his work quietly. Even though we wish he'd speak up more and explain himself.

And he is never in a hurry. Though we often wish he'd move a little faster. But, he has a process. His first strokes lay the foundation from which our lives take shape. He knows what he wants to accomplish in us. One-stroke-at-a-time.

There are times when his strokes seem straightforward, and we think we understand what he is trying to shape in us. But, other times the canvas looks muddied; we can't make heads-from-tails…and we wonder if he hasn't made a mistake somewhere along the line.

Muddied seems to be the state of my canvas of late. And there's been no explanation from heaven why on earth it is so.

When my heart grows alarmed, I call to mind my sweet, little elderly friend painting serenely in the conservatory. I remember the muddied spot, and the concern I had. Then I remember how with a single brush stroke he began to bring clarity to what I thought was a mistake and it helps me breathe when I want to panic.

This prayer written long years ago also whispers comfort to me.

> *If traces of Christ's love-artistry be upon me, may he work on with his divine brush until the complete image be obtained and I be made a perfect copy of him, My Master.*
> —Arthur Bennett

As do promises from God's love letter like…

> *As the Spirit of the Lord works within us, we become more and more like him.*
> —2nd Corinthians 3:18

And peace sweeps in.

The canvas is still muddied at the moment, but I know that God has a process. And with one stroke of his brush he can, and will one day, transform this confusing place into something beautiful, for his glory.

> *Thank you, sweetest Savior, for your love-artistry in my life. Continue working with your divine brush until I become more and more like you.*

Where on my life's canvas are the colors a little muddied? Will I trust God's divine paintbrush?

When the Enemy Steals My Pillow

Jo

My eyelids are heavy, but my thoughts are heavier.
—Unknown

I've stopped sleeping again.

It's not so much that I've consciously decided to give up this restful time, I've simply not been able to make it part of my evening repertoire. This isn't something I'm proud of. I'm not getting more done or trying to be efficient with my time. My closets aren't more organized. My Tupperware drawer is still a mess. I simply cannot get to sleep and stay asleep. No amount of warm milk, sleep aids, or reruns of old sitcoms can get me to settle in for a good night's slumber.

Instead, I worry.

I worry for our world. There is so much pain going on around us.

I worry for my kids, especially my soon-to-be high schooler. So many changes are happening for him right now. Pressure for school is mounting. Commitment for sports is unyielding. Attention from girls is escalating. I feel him slipping from my arms and from my influence. My role as a Mom is changing every day and it's all so new for me. The pressure is overwhelming to shape this young man to make wise decisions, to call on the name of the Lord for guidance, and to honor others in his quest to live his own unique life.

Even though I know I shouldn't, I worry.

The Lord knew we would worry. And, he expressly tells us not to. In Matthew 6:11, Jesus tells us to pray, "Give us this day our daily bread." Daily bread. Not tomorrow's bread, or bread for next week. He provides the bread we need today. And that means we need to trust that he will do the same tomorrow and every day following. He doesn't want us to worry.

The reference to bread came many years before when the Israelites were wandering through the desert on their way to the Promised Land. Food was scarce in the desert, so God told Moses that he would provide it. And so he miraculously made food fall from the sky. Every morning a fresh layer of "manna" lay on the ground. Daily bread. They couldn't store it for tomorrow. They just had to wait for the next day's provision. They weren't supposed to worry.

Jesus' disciples worried too. They worried about their own provision. They worried about tomorrow. They worried what would happen to them once Jesus left this world.

In Matthew 6:25, Jesus tells them, "Therefore I tell you, do not worry about your life, what you will eat or drink; or about your body, what you will wear. Is not life more than food, and the body more than clothes?"

Jesus continued to tell them that he would provide what they needed, when they needed it. The whole time he was with them, he kept showing them they could trust him. He provided healing to those who needed it, regardless of the day or time that others might have expected him to do so. He provided food to the hungry even when the circumstances were grim. And he provides for our daily needs as well. Worry has no place in the mind of one who can learn to trust him.

So, as I lay awake, I recite his words, and I pray the worry will subside.

Are you tired? Worn out? Burned out on religion? Come to me. Get away with me and you'll recover your life. I'll show you how to take a real rest. Walk with me and work with me—watch how I

do it. Learn the unforced rhythms of grace. I won't lay anything
heavy or ill-fitting on you. Keep company with me and you'll
learn to live freely and lightly.
—Matthew 11:28-29 (MSG)

And so, I vow not to worry. Freely and lightly sounds much better, at least until tonight.

Do I recognize God's faithfulness and power in all areas of my life?

Our Best-Laid Plans

Julie

It's plain and simple, life or the plans we
make in life are not plain or simple.
—Unknown

I had spent countless hours on the internet pouring over airline, hotel and B&B sites for our trip to France. Starting the process in February, booking our flights the end of April, and our hotels the end of May.

But, even best-laid plans can change at a moment's notice.

Our flight was delayed two hours in Minneapolis. The connecting flight in Frankfurt—missed. Confusion and mayhem ensued. Long lines were endured, *barely*. When we finally arrived in Geneva hours later, Rey's bag had gone AWOL, literally—even the airline had no idea where it was.

And to top it all off, Rey was scheduled to start work at a cheese factory in the Alps the next day. Only, his uniforms and boots were packed in that lost suitcase—floating somewhere out there in the airport stratosphere.

Here's the thing I'm learning through experiences like this one… God doesn't always get you where you are going to *smoothly*.

But, I like things to go smoothly. In fact, I kind of expect it to. How about you? If you're like me, interruptions, schedule changes, waiting in long lines, or behind slow cars in the fast lane when you're in a hurry can be a real mood-changer.

Why is that, I wonder? It's not as if everything in life falls into place or goes according to our plans and dreams every single time. But somehow, we still expect it to and are so disappointed, frustrated, or agitated, even with God, when it doesn't.

What does this say about me? About us? What does this say about our faith in a God who works all things together for our good? (Romans 8:28)

Our arrival in France put us behind schedule in every way. With no way of connecting with *le fromager* (the cheese-maker) in Bogeve, we headed to our B&B on Lake Geneva. The following day we nervously made our way to our hotel in La Chappelle d'Abondance and prayed for the best.

As we meandered the streets of La Chappelle to get to know our little home-away-from-home, we "happened upon" a *Fruitere* (cheesemaking facility). And that *Fruitere* just "happened" to be one connected to Rey's contact, Joël.

After a brief phone conversation between Samuel, the plant manager in La Chapelle, and Joël, it was decided that Rey should start there before transferring to the larger facility in Bogeve.

Yes! He ended up having to work in street clothes for a couple of days. And yes! They and his shoes were a mess. But, before long Rey and his missing-in-action suitcase were reunited after a trip back to Geneva was made to retrieve it. And from that day forth Rey was fully garbed for duty.

But, the sweetest part of this story is that had the trip gone as we had planned, had Rey connected with Joël from the start, and had he gone to work first in Bogeve…he might not have had an easy go of it.

And I believe God knew that.

God knew that flight delays, missed flights, and lost suitcases, were exactly what was required to give Rey the most precious gift to a cheesemakers heart…the gift of communicating and understanding the process of making something he is so passionate about—*fromage alpin*—Alpine cheese!

God knew that by working side-by-side, one-on-one with Samuel, who was able to speak broken English, Rey would learn technical French cheese-making terms that would enable him to communicate with the non-English-speaking staff at the factory in Bogeve.

We couldn't see it at the time. Or understand it. But, God did. In spite of what seemed like a series of disasters in the beginning, the Savior had been working even in those for our good.

Perhaps this life you're living isn't at all that you imagined or planned for. Perhaps it feels like it's all going a bit sideways for you. Or for a loved one. One disaster followed by another. And you wonder where in the world God is in it all.

I've been there. In fact, I'm there now. Wondering.

But if there's one thing I do know in the midst of best-laid plans gone awry, God is, and will, work these days into something good for his glory.

> *Anything under God's control is never out of control.*
> —Charles Swindoll

> *I know that your goodness and love will be with me all my life…*
> —Psalm 23:6 (GNT)

What might God be asking me to entrust to him? Even when life looks upside down?

Trusty Old Cart

LuAnn

Before your worries make you weary or your concerns get consuming, I pray that you will recognize what is happening and ask Jesus to give you a resting place for your restless heart... Remember who God is—and how good He is at being God.
—Renee Swope

"Sir, can I help you with that?!" I asked as I walked across the road. I had been enjoying quiet time at the prayer cabin's dock on Spirit Lake when I heard some clattering behind me. I turned and noticed an elderly man slowly loading 12-pack after 12-pack of pop from his truck in his garage onto a wheeled cart.

As I got closer I asked again. This time he heard me and looked up. "Ah no. I'm fine, mam. Got this here trusty cart. I used to unload each of these cases by hand and then carry them into the house. Then I thought, how silly is that? I have a perfectly good cart that is sitting by the garage wall doing nothing. It's so easy now. I just load up the cart, and away we go into the house and down the stairs!"

"Down the stairs?!" I asked incredulously. "That can't be easy! Are you sure you don't want help? It's no problem at all."

"No. It really is easy with this here cart. I can work hard or hardly work, and at my age, I choose the latter. And this cart sure makes it easy!" he said with a pleased grin that matched the sunny yellow color of his rambler.

"Well, that's still pretty impressive. And a smart idea. Have a good day!" I called out as I left the man in the red, white, and blue plaid shirt to continue to load up his beloved cart.

Later when I was back at the cabin reading in God's Word and reflecting on the day, a thought struck me. I realized we often are like that man and his cart. And what we have is so much more than a cart.

For those of us that have trusted in Christ's saving power, we have the Holy Spirit living in us, ready to guide us, to help us, to make this life of ours that is filled with trials easier to bear—giving us peace and joy in the midst of them. (1 Thessalonians 1:6 and Romans 15:13)

But with the world's many distractions, and with our tendency to want to take control and solve things ourselves, we leave the Holy Spirit along the walls of our lives unused. *We forget the power we have residing right in us.*

What is it you need to put on the Holy Spirit's cart? What worry, crossroad, fear, ministry, plan, goal, or disappointment? God through you is more than able.

Maybe it is a heavy burden. Jesus says, "Come to me, all you who are weary and burdened, and I will give you rest." Matthew 11:28

One of the burdens I think we often carry is our burden in trying to win God's approval. But Jesus gives us rest from this—the work to make us right before a holy God has been done for us by Jesus. We need to stop trying to please God and start living under the freedom we have in Christ. After we come to him expressing our belief in his saving grace, our striving to measure up can be done. When we fully grasp God's amazing gift to us, it is life-changing, and our "works" come from this overflow (Colossians 3:12). Anything else will frustrate and burden us.

Jesus replied, "And you experts in the law, woe to you, because you load people down with burdens they can hardly carry, and you yourselves will not lift one finger to help them." (Luke 11:46)

And Paul says, "It is the freedom that Christ has set us free. Stand firm, then, and do not let yourselves be *burdened* again by a yoke of slavery." (Galatians 5:1) "God made you alive with Christ. He forgave us all our sins, having canceled the written code with its regulations that was against us and that stood opposed to us; he took it away, nailing it to the cross." (Colossians 2:13b-14)

You are indeed free and loved in Christ my friend! Unload the burden of not feeling like what you do ever measures up.

If you find yourself in a season where you carry a burden that is so heavy you can't even seem to find your cart, it is okay. Keep searching. God is faithful.

And sometimes you need to let your brothers and sisters in Christ know. The older I get, the quicker I am to get out my phone and start contacting my prayer warrior family and friends.

And if you are not in that season, look around. Someone may need to borrow your cart. Someone may need "Jesus with skin on." That is how the church is supposed to operate: "Carry each other's burdens, and in this way, you fulfill the law of Christ." (Galatians 6:2)

We live in a sin-soaked world with an enemy that is jealous of Christ and our glory in Christ. He wants our defeat (Ephesians 6:10-12). We defeat Satan and his lies by remembering that Christ is in us and for us, and that as the *body of Christ,* we are even stronger.

Our heavenly Father, when my arms become weary, may I remember sooner rather than later, that I need to stop carrying the burden on my own. You are our burden-bearer. And thank you for the precious saints you have placed in my life. Help me to have eyes for those who are about to be pulled over with their burden and the best way that I can help. We love because you love, and your love, power, and guidance lives in us! We praise you, for you are worthy!

I keep asking that the God of our Lord Jesus Christ, the glorious Father, may give you the Spirit of wisdom and revelation, so that you may know him better. I pray also that the eyes of your heart may be enlightened in order that you may know the hope to which he has called you, the riches of his glorious inheritance in the saints, and his incomparably great power for us who believe.
—Ephesians 1:17-19

Those who know your name trust you, O Lord, because you have never deserted those who seek your help.
—Psalm 9:10

Oh, how the world needs to see, feel, and experience Jesus! God wants to give us confidence in Christ that others can see, so they will want Him for themselves. It's time that we, God's girls, let Jesus have His way in our lives. Let's make a promise that every time doubt casts its shadow over us, we will run back to Jesus, turn toward the light, and stand in the shadow of the cross where everything changes.
—Renee Swope

What burden do I need to stop carrying on my own?

Discovering Our Worth

How Sweet It Isn't

Jo

Wanting to be someone else is a waste of the person that you are.

—Marilyn Monroe

It happened once again, that all-too-familiar conversation I had with a friend of mine who had found herself in a complex situation. She had let someone take advantage of her good nature and she didn't know how to dig out of the hole in which she had found herself. She had tried to have a conversation with the offending person, tried to right the wrong, but to no avail.

So, she called me. After listening to her issue and offering some suggestions on how to fix the problem, she thanked me for my time and said, "I just wish I was more like you. You're just so tough."

People started calling me "tough" way back in junior high school. I wasn't tough in the strong sense, just tough in the "I don't take any guff" kind of sense. I've always wondered where that tough exterior, that no-nonsense type of personality comes from. Like most behavior traits, I assumed it was born out of my family structure. Growing up with three brothers and no sisters, I was kind of on my own to either stand up and be counted, or sulk back and be belittled. I feel like I chose sulking more often than standing, but maybe my perception was a little off.

I loved debate and persuasive speaking. I enjoyed putting together (and winning) arguments of any kind. My high school teachers encouraged me to become a lawyer. At my wedding rehearsal dinner, the advice my brothers gave to my future husband (in front of everyone) was, "Don't wrong her. It won't go well for you."

I was the girl in 9th grade whom other girls would elect to stand up for a friend who was being bullied. I was the girl who was coaxed by her friends to tell a teacher how unfair his grading was. I was the one my siblings would elect to ask mom or dad permission to do something they knew we weren't allowed to do.

Tough? I don't know if that's the right word, but I've never much liked it as a descriptor.

To be honest, I'd rather be sweet.

Sweet is defined as: having the pleasant taste characteristic of sugar or honey; not salty, sour, or bitter.

When people call a Christian *sweet*, it usually means they reek of God's goodness, that they embody the graciousness of Christ. They hug. Their eyes sparkle. Goodness spills out of them like water from a gushing hose. I know these women. I love being around these women. I wish I could be more like these women. They give without reservation. They encourage without judgment. They love unconditionally and unreservedly. They always have an encouraging word and apply an appropriate Scripture passage to the situation.

Sweet.

I should be sweet. But I'm not.

I wish I was the person people call when they need some encouragement rather than the person they call when they need some courage. I'd rather be the person that someone asks to hold their hand through a trial rather than the person that they call to walk ahead of them and push aside their tormentors in a battle.

And while I appreciate being the rescuer…while I love being out doing battle for my friends, sometimes in the quiet of the night, I whisper to myself, "I wish I was sweet."

What kind of word would you put in the blank?

I wish I was more _____.

I wish I was more like _____.

I wish I could do _____ better.

It's so tempting to wish away the strengths God has given us in favor of the strengths we see in others. But God knew what he was doing with each one of us, right from the start.

> *You made all the delicate, inner parts of my body and knit me together in my mother's womb. Thank you for making me so wonderfully complex! Your workmanship is marvelous—how well I know it. You watched me as I was being formed in utter seclusion, as I was woven together in the dark of the womb. You saw me before I was born. Every day of my life was recorded in your book. Every moment was laid out before a single day had passed.*
> —Psalm 139:13-16 (NLT)

Maybe personality traits are part of the knitting-together. Perhaps a desire for a change in temperament is to speak against what God has created and recorded for each one of us. I love how author Sheri Rose Shepherd imagines God reflecting on his created beings:

> *I love what I have created. I am delighted in you! You never need to pretend to be something other than who I made you to be. I gave my life for you so you could live free to be yourself. Never again doubt who you are, why you are here, and how much you are loved.*
> —Sheri Rose Shepherd

I'm not sweet. But God is willing to work within my limitations. After all, he made me limited so that I could find completion in him.

He who began a good work in you will carry it on to completion
until the day of Christ Jesus.
—Philippians 1:6

What is one of the strengths God has given me that I don't always appreciate?

Lost

Julie

I'm lost
I've gone to look for myself
If I get back before I return
Please ask me to wait!
—Unknown

Our last day in Aix en Provence happened to be Market Day. And I, for one, was not leaving until I had sufficiently shopped as many stalls as possible.

Nearly every inch of those tight, old Roman city streets was lined with vendors plying their wares.

We began our little spree amidst the artfully displayed tables piled high with veggies of every shape and variety. Little chalkboards with the prices in Euros were wedged between purple *l'aubergine* (eggplant), bright red tomatoes, orange peppers and bundles of *laitue* (lettuce).

From there we made our way over to the local *les fromagers* (cheesemakers) who were offering small wedges to taste, and to the meat merchants slicing slivers of *saucisson* for sampling. And who in their right mind would pass up the wine vendors? A sip of summer rosé does a heart good.

Then there were the stands of fresh cut flowers—big bouquets of *les tournesols* (sunflowers), peonies and roses, as well as plants to add to one's garden. I could've stayed there all day, but a booth filled with homemade soaps of jasmine, cherry blossom, *vanille*, and nearly every fragrance under the sun, tempted me to move on. That was followed by a stall filled with all things *lavende* (lavender).

The deeper we went into the market, the greater the hordes of humanity. Temps were nearing 100°—the humidity was thick.

And I loved it! Absolute joy.

That is until…

Having forgotten something back at the B&B, Rey turned to me and said, "I'll run quick and meet you back here." I replied, "No problem, I'll just meander around in the general vicinity, and from your 6'7" height advantage, I will spot you or you will spot me."

I puttered nonchalantly through sweet little canopied shops filled with the latest styles the women of France were wearing. I perused purse shops and checked out tables full of sandals.

But, an hour later there was still no sight of him.

As the heat intensified...so were my concerns.

Rey wasn't using his cell phone due to the high cost of roaming charges, so I figured my only option was to make my way back across town to the B&B to see what the holdup was. Arriving there, I learned that he had long since come and gone. I turned on my heel with just a "hint" of agitation and trudged back to the *place du marché* (marketplace) under a scorching sun.

Stopping to buy a *bouteille d'eau* (bottle of water), I stationed myself in one corner of the market where I could see across it and down several streets at the same time, while I searched for a fair-haired tall man amongst the crowds. But, to no avail.

I finally decided to go once more in search of him—up and down those congested streets.

By afternoon the heat had gotten oppressive. I was drenched in sweat and feeling faint. All I could do was keep moving, keep praying, keep repeating, *"When I am afraid I will trust in you,"* (Psalm 56:3) and keep looking up over the crowds for a glimpse of that tall hubby of mine.

As two and a half hours passed to three, it finally dawned on me to go to the parking garage. "If nothing else," I thought, "I'll wait for him by the car."

Plodding my way slowly through the marketplace crowds, block-after-block, I finally reached our favorite *boulangerie* (bakery) near the car park.

Just then, Rey rounded the corner. If I had had an ounce of strength left, I would have given him a piece of my mind. But, I was just so thankful to see him, I could only feel relief.

It's amazing how the sensation of wonderment and pure delight that I once felt in the marketplace shifted so quickly and dramatically when I realized something was amiss. All I could think about from that point on was one thing...to be found.

But, you don't have to be in a crowd like that to feel lost.

Awhile back I asked a gal standing in line ahead of me at the grocery store what the Chinese symbol meant that was tattooed on her shoulder. She turned around and said, "Lost."

I didn't know how to respond. I left the store with a sinking heart, lifting prayers heavenward for that precious gal and pleading with God to "find" her.

Not many of us tattoo our sense of hopelessness, our feelings of despair, our longing to be found, on our shoulders. But, God sees it written on our faces, across our hearts and in our thoughts.

If that's you, dear friend, please remember this…

You may feel lost and alone, but God knows exactly where you are.

Whether we are lost in Aix or lost in spirit, we are never lost to God.

Jesus told them this parable: "Suppose someone among you had one hundred sheep and lost one of them. Wouldn't he leave the other ninety-nine in the pasture and search for the lost one until he finds it? And when he finds it, he is thrilled and places it on his shoulders. When he arrives home, he calls together his friends and neighbors, saying to them, 'Celebrate with me because I've found my lost sheep.'"
—Luke 15:3-6

When was the last time I felt lost? Or do I know someone who is? How can I help them understand that they are not alone?

Seeking Jesus

LuAnn

The Lord looks down from heaven on all mankind to see if there are any who understand, any who seek God.
—Psalm 14:2

He rewards those who earnestly seek him.
—Hebrews 11:6b

Two young teen friends spent months on their outfits. They had heard that the more noticeable the outfit, the better chance of getting stage-side viewing of their favorite performer at her concert. One of the moms—a friend of mine—was a little skeptical all this work would pay off.

But, the girls believed. So they spent hours sewing taffeta, lights and various baubles and trinkets onto their outfits in an effort to stand out, to get noticed.

And it paid off.

As they were enjoying the night, the mother of the performing artist took notice of them and said the words the teen girls worked so hard to hear, "Come with me."

They didn't look back. In fact, they quickly left their moms behind sitting speechless in their balcony seats, as they quickly and excitedly made their way up front.

In the book of Luke, we find Zacchaeus exhibiting the same kind of urgency (19:1-10). He wanted to see Jesus. And he wanted a front-row seat.

But, Zacchaeus had many obstacles to overcome; he was not well-liked as a chief tax collector, and he was a small man in a big crowd. His odds were not in his favor.

Can you remember a situation where you felt like the odd-man-out? I sure have.

But, Zacchaeus didn't let that stop him. Luke reports in 19:4, "So he ran ahead and climbed a sycamore-fig tree to see him."

Think of the scene for a moment. You are in a crowd trying to watch for someone who is quickly becoming famous—his unconventional ways and astounding miracles are often in the news—and he will be passing closely by. You are getting pushed and shoved. Amongst the chaos, you happen to see movement in a tree up ahead. You squint your eyes against the sun expecting to see a busy squirrel, but as your eyes finally focus in, instead of a squirrel or a daring adolescent, you see a full-aged man hanging out in a tree.

This is where we find Zacchaeus. He was going to do what he could to see Jesus.

Dr. Marcellino D'Ambrosia states, "The tug that Zacchaeus felt inside was the grace of God drawing him to his Son."

And what happened next had to be beyond his imagination. For not only did Zacchaeus get to see Jesus as he hung out in that tree, Jesus *noticed him*; Jesus looked up and said, "Zacchaeus, come down immediately. For I'm going to your house today."

Can you imagine Zacchaeus' great surprise? And, since Jews hated tax collectors because they were dishonest employees of the oppressive Roman government, can you hear the shocked whispers and groans, the staccato-like disapproving *tsks* drifting in the crowd? Why would Jesus want to associate with Zacchaeus of all people? Luke reports, "All the people saw this and began to mutter, "He has gone to be the guest of a sinner.""

(Luke 19:7) *(Do you hear the undercurrents of a little jealousy perhaps?)*

Thankfully, though, Jesus never let others' distaste of whom he hung out with change how he operated. Jesus continually shocked people with whom he talked with, reached out to, and connected with.

They were not usually the famous, well-connected or those with multiple Bible degrees.

Instead, they were people who were humble, were aware of their sin and who knew and recognized who had the answer. They often were the ones who sought him out. They were the ones who responded to his calling.

They were people like Zacchaeus. So, let's look at the rest of the story:

> *So, Zacchaeus came down at once and welcomed him gladly...he stood up and said to the Lord, "Look, Lord! Here and now I give half of my possessions to the poor, and if I have cheated anybody out of anything, I will pay back four times the amount." Jesus said to him, "Today salvation has come to this house, because this man, too, is a son of Abraham. For the Son of Man came to seek and to save the lost."*
> —Luke 19:6,8-10

Zacchaeus encountered Jesus and was forever changed.

Like Zacchaeus, when we truly meet Jesus, we rightly see *who* we are...and *how* we are... And when we repent, we are forever changed.

> *Therefore, if anyone is in Christ, the new creation has come: The old has gone, the new is here!*
> —2 Corinthians 5:17

Zacchaeus could have let his sins, his reputation, and his lowly stature stop him from seeking Jesus and from responding to his call, but he didn't.

And just like Zacchaeus, Jesus promises us that when we seek him, we will find him.

> *You will seek me and find me when you seek me with all your heart.*
> *—Jeremiah 29:13*

> *So, I say to you...seek and you will find; knock and the door will be opened to you.*
> *—Luke 11:9*

His eyes are on you. His hand is outstretched. He says to you, "I see you. Come down. I'm coming over."

Dear heavenly Father, help us to put aside any pride, love of our sin, busyness, or feelings of unworthiness and seek you earnestly. We thank you that you promise if we seek you, we will find you and that your passion is to seek and save those of us that are lost.

What may be keeping me from fully seeking Jesus?

Stay-At-Home Mom vs. Working Mom

Heidi

Therefore, since we are surrounded by such a huge crowd of witnesses to the life of faith, let us strip off every weight that slows us down, especially the sin that so easily trips us up. And let us run with endurance the race God has set before us. We do this by keeping our eyes on Jesus, the champion who initiates and perfects our faith. Because of the joy awaiting him, he endured the cross, disregarding its shame. Now he is seated in the place of honor beside God's throne.
—Hebrews 12:1-2

I think back to when I bumped into a friend at the mall just days before my maternity leave was over. With her own baby on hip, my stay-at-home-mom friend explained she needed some fresh air—and what better place than among the clothing racks, shoe sales, and hubbub of other SAHMs looking to get out of the house.

I just stared at her. Her life seemed so carefree. Anyone passing by would covet (what looked to be) a life full of free afternoons and minimal stress. But within *how are you's, you look so good, and give me life updates*, she pulled me in between clearance racks and divulged. (That's what we do, you know. We women can't help where we are. If there's secret confessions to be made, we will SPILL… Even if it means hiding under hangers.)

My dear friend grabbed my shirt, her toddler started screaming, and her shoulders collapsed. She said, to be honest, some days are hard. Many are lonely. And sometimes she just wishes to be back at work, enjoying a lunch with her colleagues and feeling accomplished by a marked-up to-do list. Doing something for HER for once.

Later, I bumped into another friend who returned back to her office, briefcase, and dress suits after spending months at home with her kid. Another round of *how are you's, you look so good, and give me life updates*. All the same, she spilled the beans. "It doesn't help when he screams at daycare drop-off," she permits. "That can make anyone cringe–but as I sit in meetings, I'm wondering how he's waking up from naptimes and looking up to an unfamiliar face. Wondering why it's not mom." The worst– those days when she comes home late just in time to put him down for bed; she wonders if it's worth it.

Both situations are completely understandable, common. Even predictable. You want to be there to witness every major milestone in your baby's childhood, and you can't imagine sharing the responsibility of raising your child with someone else. I'm nodding right along with you. But there's a pull to follow your dreams, pay the bills, and/or get some social time (aka me time) for your extroverted self. I'm still nodding. Which to choose?

As a mom who went back to work and now as a mom who stays at home, I've learned two things:

The grass is always greener on the other side. The stay-at-home moms feel like they're always "on" with no breaks, may go insane if conversation doesn't go beyond *goo-goo ga-ga*, and can't help but partly miss their powerhouse heels and impressive email signature. Working moms feel guilty for missing their child's day-to-day affairs, frazzled from running here to there, and torn between that work-life balance that seems despairingly impossible.

Comparison kills contentment. Staying home isn't an option because your mortgage would drown a single-person income.

But when you log onto Facebook only to see so-and-so post pics of her home life plus baby, jealousy rages, and you maybe, sort of (ugly) cry a little. Or you miss the benefits of work and accomplishing something other than getting in the shower and putting the baby down successfully; and when your sister celebrates a promotion, you wonder if you're maximizing your own potential…or letting it fall by the wayside.

Solution? *Fix your eyes on the race set before you.* In a race, it would be foolish to take off running looking at the sprinter to your left. The course set before you may zigzag, turn, or cross over, but if you're gawking at another runner, you may trip, miss the finish line, or forfeit the medal completely.

In the same way, God has a unique plan for each of us–some moms, that means staying at home, and for others, that involves working–and instead of stumbling around with envy or getting tripped up by discontentment, he asks us to turn our gaze upward, grit our teeth, and press on to endure the race set before us. Not the race set before your neighbor mom who works full-time or your actual mom who stayed home. But your race. Which, by the way, is bound to be beautiful because it's tailor-made by a God who withholds no good thing from you. Take heart that it may be tough now, but in the end, it's promised to be so worth it.

So, fix your eyes today, mama. Believe you me, you won't want to miss the glory of what God has for you in the course ahead.

Whether it's someone else's house, family, job, or income level, how am I most tempted to compare my life with others? What would it look like to choose contentment?

Discovering Prayer and Solitude

Rooftop Refuge

Julie

How lovely is your dwelling place, O Lord. How I long to be there, my soul faints to enter...
—Psalm 84:1-2

On the roof, it's peaceful as can be and there the world below don't bother me...
—Carole King

It was hotter than blazes the five days we made Aix-en-Provence our home. I was sure I would melt into a puddle and be remembered no more. Especially after a day of exploring ancient Aix's compact, often confusing and extremely congested streets, packed with visitors, like ourselves, converging there for a piece of its beauty and mystique.

At day's end, we would slowly mount four flights of stairs to our little apartment up on the roof. Each step we took felt heavier than the last; doubts crept in that I would reach the top. But, fortunately, our sweet little abode had air conditioning, a rarity in France. And nothing felt quite so wonderful as stepping through that door.

But, being cooped up in air conditioning all evening didn't suit a romantic soul like mine, either.

Gratefully, just outside our French doors was a little rooftop refuge, a perch at trees top, my very own balcony sanctuary.

So, after a nice cool shower, I'd slip out onto the porch in my jammies—with my journal and cup of tea in hand—just as the sun was slipping further west and the heat of the day lessened. What a gift it was sitting peacefully above the hubbub, listening contentedly to conversations, and watching all the comings and goings of folks as they dined in cafés and ambled their way through the narrow streets below.

Those were sacred hours for me. Gifts of all sorts were bestowed there by God. From Holy Spirit whisperings on the wind, to rest for my aching, weary feet, to sweet birdsong, to the setting sun painting the sky in pale shades of pink, orange, yellow and purples just above tiled rooftops each evening–that no doubt inspired many an artist's paintbrush down through the millennia.

But, I wasn't the only one who sought shelter above the noise and hubbub of the world below. The skyline of Aix was literally dotted with rooftop retreats of every shape and size. Shuttered windows, flung open to let the evening breezes blow through, had pots with herbs and flora tucked just outside into whatever little niche could be found at roof's edge. Any space that could be transformed into livable space was complete with table, chairs and flower pots.

As I gazed out on all those safe havens above the city, Psalm 84:1-3 came to mind.

> *How lovely is your dwelling place, O Lord. How I long to be there, my soul faints to enter... Even the sparrow has found a home and the swallow a nest for herself in your presence. How blessed they are to live and sing there!*

I picked up my journal and wrote: "*Seeking shelter from the heat of the day and the hubbub of the world seems to come naturally to us no matter where we live. But, I can't help but wonder if the same could be said of our longing for you, God. Does my soul...do our souls...faint to enter your presence after a wearying day? Is that my...our...first thought...to collapse into the shade of your sheltering presence?*"

Precious Father in heaven,
Thank you that you provide a "rooftop refuge" for each one of
us...physically and spiritually. May we seek solace in the days
ahead not only for our weary bodies, but, for our souls, in your
loving presence. Amen.

The Lord is your Protector.
The Lord stands by your side, shading and protecting you.
The sun cannot harm you during the day,
and the moon cannot harm you at night.
—Psalm 121:5-6

Where do I seek refuge?

Falling into Change

Jo

Autumn, the year's last, loveliest smile.
—William Cullen Bryant

This morning the sky looks different. The sun is lower and not quite as bright. There is a nip in the air. A big change is taking place, and I can't stop it…even if I wanted to.

Every October, the transformation is set into motion. In our yard, it starts with a lone maple tree, the one that soaks in the sunlight all summer long and offers a shady place for the perennials to grab shelter from the heat. As the sun angle shifts, that same statuesque tree begins to turn a beautiful crimson. I catch a glimpse of it through the window in my hallway, and I know that this wonderful summer season has come to a close, and fall is going to be rushing in before I know it.

I have always been fascinated by the changing of seasons. Maybe that is why I chose the Midwest as the place I wanted to live and work. I feel the change in the weather is also an opportunity for change in my own life, and I find myself looking forward to this seasonal change even more than maybe I should. Fall always brings hope of a spiritual reset of sorts, a time to prepare for a season of rest, and I am almost always ready for it.

I remember the lesson in Earth Science when I learned about the coloring of the leaves. I discovered that the leaves don't necessarily "change" colors as much as they "let go" of color. The beautiful green that we see all summer long is a result of the summer sun. The trees drink in the sunlight which keeps up the green. But the hues of red, and orange, and yellow are always there too. They are just hidden beneath. And when the leaves let go of the summer sun, the green fades away, allowing that beautiful color to light up the landscape. In order for the leaf to become its most beautiful, it has to quit taking in light, and allow the green to fade. The leaf has to begin to die before it becomes its most beautiful.

I, too, sometimes feel I need permission to stop taking in the light. But in my case, the light represents this running and rushing and keeping up. It's a worldly kind of façade that keeps me green and fitting in with the crowd. I long for rest, but the sun keeps coming, day after day, sometimes to the point of being relentlessly hot. So, I cover myself in busyness…hide behind the green chaos…smuggling out that orange and crimson and yellow, just waiting for the season to end.

When fall comes, I somehow feel this permission of sorts…permission to take a break from the bedlam and prepare for rest. I find this settling of my mind and heart allows me to sit quietly while my kids are at school and the golf course is closed, and I drink in something different than the bright, penetrating sun. The warmth comes from the inside, from the inner workings of the Holy Spirit. And I have to let go of the external in order for the internal to be heard. And as I listen, I feel the orange and yellow and crimson coming back to the surface. Change can be good when it's the kind of change he is orchestrating. The beauty is there the whole time, but he patiently waits for us to shut out what feeds us temporarily and drink from what nourishes us completely. It is in this season of quiet and listening that my soul seems to find its beauty again. And I look forward to what will come from this season of rest.

The Bible also references seasons as metaphors for God's perfect timing in delivering us through all of the changes in our lives. Seasons bring about blessings if we can keep doing good despite the difficult seasons that may be upon us.

And let us not grow weary of doing good, for in due season
we will reap, if we do not give up.
—Galatians 6:9

And as I grab a stocking cap and my favorite gloves, I head out for a brisk morning walk. As the crisp air fills my lungs, I breathe out that last breath of summer sun and welcome what's brewing from within. I feel the reds and oranges and yellows beneath my down vest, and I look forward to what will come shining through in the next season.

For everything there is a season and a time for every purpose
under heaven.
—Ecclesiastes 3:1

What blessings do I glean from the changing of seasons?

Holy Mystery—the Unexpected Voice of God

Julie

Who knows what God will say to me today or to you today or into the midst of what kind of unlikely moment he will choose to say it? Not knowing is what makes today a Holy Mystery...
—Fredrick Buechner

Our twisting and turning journey through the French countryside, leading to what seemed like nowhere, on little roads that one car could barely maneuver on, had my hubby on edge. But, I had so longed to visit Hautecombe Abbaye, that we pressed on.

It was an hour-and-a-half drive from our hotel in Annecy, a drive that at one point had us clinging precariously to cliffs-edge high above Lac du Bourget. I could hardly draw breath I was so enraptured by the amazing panoramic views...my hubby, on the other hand, was holding his breath and clutching the wheel for dear life. His nerves frayed, I began praying that somehow, someway, this crazy little adventure of ours *(mine!)* would be worth the effort.

Unfortunately, the road into the Abbaye narrowed significantly. When we met a few tour buses head on, it nearly put the kibosh on our expedition once and for all. But, with both vehicles riding the grassy edge with an inch or two to spare, we barely passed one another. We turned into the first parking area we could find so that Rey could loosen his tight-fisted clench on the steering wheel and finally breathe.

It wasn't until we started for the Abbaye that we realized that we were in for a bit of walk. We had parked in the lot farthest out on the property. But, the walk did us good. Besides, when in France, walking is a way of life...part of the journey.

As we made our way closer to the old Basilica we were startled to hear voices singing "10,000 Reasons," by Matt Redman...in English. It literally stopped us in our tracks. Tears still well up in my eyes just thinking about it.

Turning into the Abbaye entrance, we made a beeline for the restaurant to have a sweet, calm lunch where we *both* could enjoy the sweeping views of *Lac du Bourget*. Then, we took a magnificent hour-long guided tour of the Basilica.

During our tour, we were told that the Abbaye, growing more concerned about the spiritual vacuum they saw in their country, had made great strides over the last several years to welcome and work alongside other Christian denominations in order to reach France's youth. The voices we had heard singing on our way into the Abbaye had been hundreds of teens who were concluding a weeklong stay at an interdenomational camp hosted by the Abbaye.

Tears welled up once more and streamed down my face. Was I really hearing this correctly?

For years I have prayed for God's Spirit to move in this beautiful land that I love. For years I have wept for my precious friends who have struggled to believe that there is a God that loves them. A Savior who gave himself for the love of them.

And there we were...seeing God's Spirit moving with our own eyes and hearing voices of hope sing out.

By the time we began hiking back to our car, that narrow road that we had struggled like the dickens to navigate, was being inundated by a host of new teens that were piling in by the carloads. Van loads more were being dropped off by parents...all flooding into the Abbaye to attend a new week of camp.

In awe of what God was doing, all we could do was rejoice and say, "Let the cars come...tight squeeze and all!"

Yes God, you truly do have something on your heart you want to say to us...to show us...a holy mystery to reveal to our hearts...if our eyes and ears are open. Thank you for personally nudging me to Hautecombe Abbaye to hear with my own ears and see with my own eyes that you love this old world far more than I possibly could; that you are active even when I think you can't possibly be and that you are indeed answering our prayers beyond our wildest imagining.

Speak, Lord. Your servant is listening.
—1ˢᵗ Samuel 3:9b

Today *is* a Holy Mystery. What might God be trying to say to me?

Express Yourself

LuAnn

Come to Me with your defenses down, ready to be blessed and filled with My Presence. Relax, and feel the relief of being totally open and authentic with Me. You have nothing to hide and nothing to disclose, because I know everything about you already. You can have no other relationship like this one. Take time to savor its richness, basking in my golden light.
—Sarah Young

I was babysitting my dear six-month-old grandniece the other evening. She's in that fun exploring and discovery stage. One of her discoveries of great interest that night was her voice. Noelle was trying everything from raspberries, to clucking, to high falsettos, to delighted squeals and giggles. She was telling me many stories and was quite pleased with her many sounds. And I was enjoying the "conversations" as well.

Later, she tried out another voice…one that let me know she was not too pleased with me and this bedtime thing. Here's my interpretation of what she was trying to tell me, "Auntie, I have more exploring to do. Let me out of here right now! I mean, really… right now! Don't you dare sit and enjoy that mocha latte during my distress!"

No hinting around there. She expressed herself loud and clear. She wasn't afraid to cry out.

I have always been drawn to people who can express themselves...that's probably why David has always been one of my favorite Bible characters. Yes, the throw-the-stones-round-and-round, giant-killer David. And, although I love that story and its amazing lessons, what blesses me at heart-level is his expressive communication with God in the Psalms.

David talks to God *a lot*…and about almost everything. This shows the intimate relationship he had with God. This is probably one of the reasons he is able to tell us so much *about* God. It took me the better part of a day at a prayer cabin once taking notes on all he had to say about God: majestic, great, gracious, righteous, slow to anger, rich in love, compassion on all he has made, good, upright, creator of all, our shield, fortress, rock, saves and guides the humble…to name just a few.

Learning and reflecting on God's qualities was important to David and led him to often praise God for who he is. I also think understanding God so well led him to such authentic communication with him.

Like these *bold requests*:

> *Remember not the sins of my youth and my rebellious ways* (25:7). *Show me your ways* (25:4). *Turn away my eyes from looking at vanity* (119:36). *Oh Lord, be not far off; O my strength, come quickly to help me* (22:19).

And this leads me to what I love about David most—when David was anxious, distressed, doubtful, or downcast, he let God know about it:

> *Evening, morning, and noon I cry out in distress* (55:17a). *I say to God my Rock, 'Why have you forgotten me? Why must I go about mourning, oppressed by the enemy?'* (42:9). *Turn to me and be gracious to me, for I am lonely and afflicted. The troubles of my heart have multiplied; free me from my anguish* (25:17). *Why, O Lord, do you stand far off? Why do you hide yourself in times of trouble* (10:1)?

Have we not all felt this way at times?

I know I have. But, often I stuff these feelings instead of expressing them to God because it makes me feel unholy somehow.

And sometimes I simply hide them out of pride. I like to have it all together. I think I should be joyful, peaceful, and trusting 100 percent of the time, and as a Christ-follower, anything other than that feels like pure evil. So, I pretend all is well.

Which is ridiculous, really. God is all-knowing; it isn't like he doesn't see what's going on inside of me.

It reminds me of an old photo of when I was little. I was sitting on the white linoleum kitchen floor of our farm house with my crochet blanket over me, and my mom was standing right there looking at me. But I thought I was being so smart, hiding in plain sight like the invisible man.

It's odd, isn't it? Authenticity is one of the qualities we value most in others, but, somehow, we feel we must act differently with God.

David, on the other hand, was brutally honest before God, and believed that God would hear him and respond:

> *The Lord is near to all who call on him, to all who call on him in truth* (145:18). *He is close to the brokenhearted and saves those who are crushed in spirit* (34:18). *God hears him in his distress* (55:17b).

And I think this brutal honesty is part of what brings David, and us, out of the pit, the depression, the fear, the anxiety...

We cry out, and God responds...

With his hope, his peace, his faithfulness, his promises from his Word, his guidance, or with encouragement and guidance from a fellow brother or sister in Christ...

We are reminded of his greatness, his goodness, his faithfulness and his love, and our souls right themselves once more.

And we praise him for who he is.

When Noelle was crying out in anger and distress, guess what? I responded. Not right away. Not probably in the timing she would have liked. But I did come and "rescue her." And she fell asleep peacefully soon after.

God does the same for you. He does the same for me. So, cry out to God. It's okay.

> *For you, Lord, have never forsaken those who seek you.*
> —Psalm 9:10b

> *I sought the Lord, and he answered me; he delivered me from all my fears. Those who look to him are radiant.*
> —Psalm 34:4, 5a

> *Because you are my help, I sing in the shadow of your wings.*
> —Psalm 63:7

What do I need to get honest with God about?

Metamorphosis

Julie

*We seem so frightened today of being alone that we never let it
happen. It is a difficult lesson to learn–to leave one's friends and
family and deliberately practice the art of solitude for an hour or
a day or a week. And yet, once it is done, I find there is a quality
to being alone that is incredibly precious.*
—Anne Morrow Lindbergh

*Early in the morning, well before sunrise, Jesus rose and went to
a solitary place where he could be alone in prayer.*
—Mark 1:35

I spent the afternoon gardening at my friend Mariann's house.
When we parted ways, she blessed me with gardening goodies.
As soon as I got home, I planted those green gifts, along with a
packet of milkweed seeds I'd purchased, to add to my growing
gardening collection of butterfly-charmers.

I love everything about butterflies–from the fuzzy caterpillar
stage to chrysalis to the final metamorphosis. That's why flowers
like allium, asters, bee balm, coneflowers, daylilies, hollyhocks,
lavender, Russian sage and Shasta daisies fill every space
possible in my garden to attract my beautiful winged friends.

> *I now notice almost every single butterfly. I pay attention
> to plain old butterflies, not just the ones in tiaras or argyle
> socks. Butterflies…are like one perfect teaspoon of
> creation.*
> —Anne Lamott

For all the enjoyment fuzzy caterpillars and flittering butterfly antics bring, it's the cocoon stage that absolutely intrigues me. I find it nothing short of *supernatural!* How God takes a hairy little creature with myriad legs and transforms it in the quiet darkness of a chrysalis into a winged thing of beauty–in just a week or two–flabbergasts me.

And yet, astonishingly enough, that very miracle of transformation that God shapes in a cocoon, he also longs do in us.

But, *that* kind of work requires something of *us*.

It requires our time. Just as the weaving of a caterpillar into a butterfly takes time.

In order for God to do that kind of supernatural metamorphosis in our lives, we must carve out time hidden away from all eyes but his. Time alone. Time in solitude. Time enough to free us from distractions. Time enough to abandon ourselves to the Spirit in order to stretch, mold and shape God's heart in us.

> *Solitude is not simply a means to an end. Solitude is its own end. It is the place where Christ remodels us in his image and frees us from the victimizing compulsions of the world. In solitude, our heart of stone can be turned into a heart of flesh, a rebellious heart into a contrite heart, and a closed heart into a heart that opens itself up once more.*
> —Henri J. Nouwen

Will you follow God's invitation to cocoon away with him somewhere quiet, perhaps for a day or two, so that he can have his way with you?

> *Making a cocoon and the transformation that goes on inside it involves weaving an environment of prayer, but not the sort of prayer we usually think of. No, this is something mysteriously different. This prayer isn't about*

talking and doing and thinking. It's about postures.
Postures of the spirit. It's turning oneself upside down so
that everything is emptied out and God can flow in. We
place ourselves in postures of the heart, in the stillness
that enables us to become aware of what God is doing, so
that we can gradually say yes to it with our whole being.
—Sue Monk Kidd

The best place I know of to cocoon alone with God is a little
prayer cabin in the middle of a Wisconsin woods. There, in the
silence, I wait. There in the solitude, God begins the process of
cleansing, shifting and redesigning my life, my heart and my
attitude.

Waiting with God. Tough? Yes. But a tough sacred
wonder!
—Annie Dillard

I'll never forget the first time I experienced that tough sacred
wonder.

I was preparing to speak at an upcoming retreat weekend and
thought the best plan would be to spend a few days at a prayer
cabin.

I arrived at the office with bags packed full of books that
I planned to use for references and research. The gentlemen that
greeted me just smiled and said, "What are you here for?"

I said, "I'm speaking at a retreat and I need to write four talks."

He quietly replied, "Might I give you a suggestion? Often the
best way to go about such an endeavor is to learn to quiet
yourself and wait on God's Spirit for direction. As great as all
those resources are, the Bible is probably the only source you'll
need. I'll be praying with you as you enter into this time alone
with God."

I thought to myself. "He just doesn't understand. He's probably never spoken at a weekend retreat." And off I went.

I pulled out all the books I had brought and piled them beside me out on the little porch and set to work. I spent hours that day jotting down thoughts, ideas, quotes, etc. Then night fell. I came back inside and continued to scour through my pile of books, but, unease started to settle inside of me.

As I got ready for bed the wrestling began in earnest.

When the sun rose the following morning, I had hardly slept a wink. Exhausted, I hauled myself out of bed and started the process all over again. But, the agitation continued. So, I took a walk. I called a friend. I told her that my mind was spinning in every direction and I hadn't even gotten started on my talks. She said she'd pray for me.

Night fell once more. As I sat down in the rocking chair, I noticed a little book sitting with a Bible on the side table. So, I grabbed it, opened it and what should I read?

> *You are about to have a rendezvous, a date with Christ. For 24 hours, you are going to be alone with God and the only book you need is the Bible. Don't take any others! Once you enter the poustinia (hermitage) you do what the Spirit tells you to do. There's nothing to be anxious about.*
> —Catherine Doherty

I wept.

God had wooed me to cocoon away with him. He longed to speak into me his heart for those gals at the retreat. But, in order for him to work his supernatural metamorphosis in me, I had to relinquish all of my efforts and surrender to the process.

And that's exactly what I did. And before I knew it–thoughts began to stir and take flight.

We love the idea of being butterflies. But, it's the transformation process that doesn't sound very appealing. So, we avoid it. We're afraid of what God might want to do in us. What he might want to speak into us.

Help us, sweet Savior, to see that it is beauty that you long to develop in us. The supernatural metamorphosis of your image that you wish to shape in us. Give us the courage to seek your heart in solitude.

In stillness and simplicity
I lose myself in finding Thee

Oh Lord, you mean so much to me
In stillness and simplicity
—Michael Card

O God, we wait before you in silent praise.
—Psalm 65:1 (TLB)

When was the last time I spent significant time in solitude listening to God's heart?

Bold Prayers

LuAnn

Bold prayers honor God, and God honors bold prayers. If your prayers aren't impossible to you, they are insulting to God."
—Mark Batterson

I found a t-shirt in the laundry bin I didn't recognize the other day. I'd like to say that is unusual, but not so in our home.

Later, when my twenty-one-old daughter came into the kitchen, she said, "Mom I got a really cool t-shirt last night. I was hanging with Abby and the gang (old high school friends) and Jason said, 'This t-shirt reminds me so much of you, Mc. Always going 100 miles an hour ever since I've known you.' So I said, 'If it is so me, then I should have it. Give me the shirt, Jason.'"

So, Jason went home shirtless.

I think it was because of that conversation that later, during my devotion time, these words hit with a little more impact: "I am a God who heals. I heal broken bodies, broken minds, broken hearts, broken lives, and broken relationships. You cannot live close to Me without experiencing some degree of healing. However, it is also true that *you have not because you ask not*...there is more—much more—available to those who ask." (Sarah Young, *Jesus Calling*; James 4:2)

So I wondered, "Am I as bold as my daughter in asking for what I want? Do I boldly approach the throne of grace in prayer?" (Hebrews 4:16)

What do you need from God that you are not asking for as well dear friend?

God has chosen prayer as the channel of his blessings. So we need to pray. And we need to pray boldly.

Matthew 20:29-34 tells of the story of two blind men who shouted, "Lord, Son of David, have mercy on us!" The crowd became irritated with them and told them to be quiet, but they shouted even louder. Then Jesus stopped and asked them, "What do you want me to do for you?" Jesus forced them to define exactly what they wanted from him, even though he and everyone else knew what they needed. Jesus made them verbalize their desire and their faith.

I have been around people who have said, "I probably should pray about it, but I think God has more important things to do." Have you ever heard anyone say that? Have you ever felt that way? That in this big world with millions of people, you and your requests don't quite make God's top ten on his "to-do" list?

I think one of the keys that inspires bold prayer is knowing God intimately and realizing how much he loves you. God made you. And he loved you enough to die for you to restore relationship to him. He desires to work through you, for your fulfillment and for his glory.

Mark Batterson, pastor and author of the New York Times bestseller, *The Circle Maker,* says,

> *It is absolutely imperative that you come to terms with this simple yet life-changing truth: God is for you. If you don't believe that, then you'll pray small timid prayers; if you do believe it, then you'll pray big audacious prayers... There is nothing God loves more than keeping promises, answering prayers, performing miracles, and fulfilling dreams. That is who He is. That is what He does.*

The apostle Paul in a Roman prison, writing to the believers in Ephesus, wanted them to understand this.

*And I pray that you, being rooted and established in love,
may have power, together with all the saints, to grasp how
wide and long and high and deep is the love of Christ, and
to know this love that surpasses knowledge—that you may
be filled to the measure of all the fullness of God.*
—Ephesians 3:17-19

What else can stop us from praying boldly? I think it sometimes
stems from our pride (Psalm 10:4). We must humble ourselves
and admit our own inadequacies. That doesn't come easy, does
it?

Jim Cymbala, in *Fresh Wind, Fresh Fire*, says, "Too seldom do
we get honest enough to admit, 'Lord, I can't handle this alone.
I've just hit the wall for the thirty-second time and I need you'."

I think there is another factor that keeps us from praying bold
prayers and is one of our greatest fears, and it is this: "What if
God is silent?"

One of my favorite books, illustrated by my friend Marianne
Richmond, that I pull out now and again when I feel like my
prayers are falling on deaf ears, is *Wait* by Russell Kelfer. It
reminds me that sometimes God's answer isn't "no" but rather
"not yet" or "just wait." It reminds me that sometimes what God
wants to do in me during the wait period can be greater than the
answer itself.

We live in what I like to call, "The McDonald/SIRI" generation.
We expect our food fast. We expect answers fast. We expect all
traffic to move at utmost speed... We expect everything *fast*. We
value short-term highs. But fast is usually not best. And it is
usually not how God works.

Batterson says:

*Our generation desperately needs to rediscover the
difference between praying* for *and praying* through. *You*

intercede until God intervenes... It's circling Jericho so many times it makes you dizzy. Like the story Jesus told about the persistent widow who drove the judge crazy with her relentless requests, praying through won't take no for an answer...it's always too soon to quit praying because you never know when the wall is about to fall.

Once Jesus disciples asked him how to pray. The prayer model Jesus gave, "Our Father, who art in heaven," is infamous in almost any church and memorized by many of us as kids. But right after that Jesus told a story of a persistent friend who keeps asking a neighbor for bread and being turned away and then says: *"I tell you, though, he will not get up and give him the bread because he is his friend, yet because of the man's boldness, he will get up and give him as much as he needs."* (Luke 11:8) Jesus concludes with this:

Ask and it will be given to you; seek and you will find; knock and the door will be opened to you. For everyone who asks receives; he who seeks finds; and to him who knocks, the door will be opened. Which of you, if his son asks for bread, will give him a stone... If you then, though are evil, know how to give good gifs to your children, how much more will your Father in heaven give good gifts to those who ask him!
—Luke 11:9-13 and Matthew 7:7-11

Batterson challenges:

When was the last time you found yourself flat on your face before the Almighty? When was the last time you cut off your circulation kneeling before the Lord? When was the last time you pulled an all-nighter in prayer?... There are higher heights and deeper depths in prayer, and God wants to take you there. It will involve more sacrifice, but if you are willing to go there, you'll realize that you didn't sacrifice anything at all.

But what if the answer is actually *no* dear friend? Some of the hardest moments in life are when you've prayed hard but the answer is *no* and you don't know why.

Do you trust that God is for you even when he doesn't give you what you asked for? Do you trust that he has reasons beyond your reason? Do you trust that his plan is better than yours? (Isaiah 55:8-9; Jeremiah 29:11)

Batterson reminds us of what some of our most powerful and effective prayers can look like:

> *When you are praying the promises of God, you can pray with holy confidence... It was settled on the cross when Jesus said, 'It is finished.' It wasn't just the final installment on our sin debt; it was the down payment on all of His promises... By the most conservative estimates, there are more than three thousand promises in Scripture. By virtue of what Jesus Christ accomplished on the cross, every one of them belongs to you. Every one of them has your name on it.*

While being bold with others may get us a cool t-shirt, approaching boldly the throne of God's grace with our requests can be life-altering, for us and for others.

Our time here is short. Let's lay hold to all God has planned for us—for our joy, for our love for others, and for God's glory.

Pray continually.
—1 Thessalonians 5:17

What do I need to boldly pray for today?

Running Restless

Julie

*What do people really have after all their work and struggling
here on earth? Throughout their life, they have
frustrations...even at night their hearts are restless.*
—Ecclesiastes 2:22-23

The mountains were hemmed in by fog. The light morning
drizzle altered quickly to downpour. It was damp and dank. The
sweet little red bistro table and chairs and the red geranium
sitting on the deck alongside looked lonely as I gazed out at them
longingly. If it had been just a bit warmer, I would've ventured
out to them, but there I stayed. In where it was warm and cozy.

The fog and rain usually settled in at night in the Alps, with the
sun making its reappearance in the morning. But not that day.
That day it had its way with us...forcing us inside.

The paramount question one faces on a day like that is...will I
yield myself truly to this involuntary confinement, or will my
heart stir restless...agitated all day long... seeking a way of
escape?

In France, a rainy day is a day to putter indoors: to play cards, to
read, or to do nothing in particular but watch the raindrops fall
outside your window.

I decided to venture down to the breakfast room and get myself a
cup of tea. There I discovered a group of guests quietly sitting
around the table playing a board game...including the owners of
the Bed and Breakfast!

No restless, agitated spirits there. No disappointment over a lost alpine hike or fidgeting in the kitchen with evening supper preparation. No... tea, café, croissants and a board game were all they needed to be content.

And there was no guilt etched on their faces in this quiet pleasure either.

I thought to myself as I returned to my room, "In our country, if we aren't doing something productive, we feel guilty."

Perhaps without realizing it, we've assimilated the US Postal Service motto into our consciousness. You know the one... "Come rain, sleet, snow or hail, we deliver."

There's a certain amount of pride we feel when we don't allow anything, certainly not a downpour, to get in the way of getting things done.

Of course, there will be plenty of days when we must get things done. But what of the days when there are no obligations? *When was the last time you had one of those?*

Would you be able to relinquish yourself to stillness–to going about the day restfully? Or, would you feel agitated, looking for any excuse to escape or start a new project?

Life is slow in France. If things don't get done today, *C'est la vie!* That's life!

So, today, my friend, be it sunshine or rain, enjoy the moment. Take pleasure in the little things. *Respirez!* Just breathe!

The fathers of the church well understood the importance of what they called 'otium sanctum' (holy leisure). They knew that we cannot give ourselves to spiritual things and deepen our relationship with God if we are obsessed with a multitude of things to do and always on the go.
—Thomas Merton

True restfulness is a form of awareness, a way of being in life. It is living ordinary life with a sense of ease, gratitude, appreciation, peace and prayer. We are restful when ordinary life is enough.
—Ronald Rolheiser

When was the last time I truly rested?

Seeking Shelter

Julie

My soul is utterly frantic for that single place of perfect refuge from which I can clearly see the winds rip and hear the tempest tear, yet despite the ferocity of the tumult I rest in such sublime peace it is as if neither existed at all. And if I have not found such a place, it is because I have not yet found God.
—Craig D. Lounsbrough

Between thunderstorms, I scampered outside for a breath of fresh air…and to take a sneak peek at the state of my waterlogged gardens. There amidst the leaves and twigs littered across our yard and driveway, I spotted a sweet little birds nest lying on its side. I was grief stricken. The violent wind and rain had shaken that little shelter right out of the tree limbs.

I carefully took the nest inside and placed it on my desk in my office. Then, I made my way back out to the deck to pull my poor potted lavender plant under the eve. It, too, looked as if it had had quite enough of the wet weather and could use a bit of a reprieve.

Hoping to spend a few minutes outside journaling between storms, I set out in search of paper towels to dry off my patio table and chairs.

As I began to wipe the glass surface, I noticed a moth clinging to the underside of our table. So, I ran inside to grab my camera.

I took my insect friend's photo just as the heavens began to weep once more, sending me scurrying back inside.

Standing at my sliding glass doors I watched the heavy raindrops pour down from the sky. It felt as if the heavens were weeping both raindrops and *tears*.

With all the tragic events that have unfolded over the past year, with such hatred and division plaguing this nation of ours…is it any wonder?

I wept along with the clouds.

As the darkness and raging storm closed in, I felt claustrophobic. Like the suffocation I have felt each time I've heard news of violence repeating itself again and again across our nation. It seems that this little "nest" of ours has been shaken from its moorings and tipped on its side. And that old fight or flight instinct wells up in me.

My soul began to feel utterly frantic.

Then, somehow, through all the chaos clamoring from within and without, God's still small voice broke through, whispering…

> *My dear child, it IS dark. And the storm—it does rage fiercely. When darkness closes in…seek refuge in the shadow of my wings. (Psalm 57:1) For I am a strong tower and all who run to me are safe. (Proverbs 18:10) Remember that even the darkness is not dark to me, the night shines like day, darkness is as light to me. (Psalm 139:12) So, do not be afraid or discouraged…for this battle raging around you is not yours, but, mine! Just take up your position (in prayer) and stand firm. (2nd Chronicles 20:15 and 17) What can mortal man do to you? (Psalm 56:3) Who can separate you from my love? (Romans 8:35)*

As peace settled in my soul, thoughts of my moth friend, riding out the storm under the shelter of our tabletop, sprung back to mind. As the winds howled around him and the rain poured down mercilessly, he didn't panic. He, instead, found a perfect refuge to ride out the tempest.

I find it easier to panic in these uncertain days. To sink under the weight of this war-weary world.

But, God longs for us to come to him. To find rest in him. To leave all our cares with him. And to find peace in him, even in the midst of these pain-filled days.

> *Dear refuge of my weary soul,*
> *On thee, when sorrows rise,*
> *On thee, when waves of trouble roll,*
> *My fainting hope relies.*
> —Anne Steele

Where does your security lie? Is God your refuge, your hiding place, your stronghold, your shepherd, your counselor, your friend, your redeemer, your savior, your guide? If He is, you don't need to search any further for security.
—Elisabeth Elliot

Come to me all you who are weary and burdened, and I will give you rest.
—Matthew 11:28

Where do I turn when my soul needs soothing?

Discovering our Blind Spots

Flawed Logic

LuAnn

There is a Me that I cannot see.
—John Ortberg

He was doing it again.

The kids and I just looked at each other, laughed, and rolled our eyes and let him continue.

You see, my husband was telling someone yet again about his year off from drinking Mountain Dew.

But well, really…

About six months into his third time of trying to go off this very addictive beverage, my husband returned from our neighborhood gas station.

As he walked through the door, I heard my daughter, McKayla, say, "Oh dad…and you were doing so good! Hasn't it been about six months that you've been off?"

Brent looked at her baffled.

Mc pointed to the beverage in his hand.

"What? This?... This isn't Mountain Dew." He said.

"Isn't that a Mountain Dew *icee*?" she asked.

"Yes. But that's not the same thing," he replied.

"What?!" Mc laughed.

From the kitchen stove, I leaned back and took a peak at him standing in the mud room. He had to be messing with her I thought. I searched his expression. No. He wasn't joking.

I asked, "So, if that's not Mountain Dew, what is it then?"

"It's not the same." He insisted in all seriousness.

"Well, what is it then?"

"It's not like drinking Mountain Dew. It's an icee."

My daughter continued to laugh, highly amused at her dad and at our exchange.

I tried again. "You mean all those years when I drank Diet Coke, because I added ice, I wasn't really drinking Diet Coke? Well, how wonderful!"

Brent laughed this time. "You guys. I live with a bunch of comedians. This is not the same. I'm not drinking Mountain Dew."

I couldn't believe he really believed that, so I had to try once again making a parallel that he could grasp to reveal his ever-so flawed logic. "So really, it is just some other syrup in the icee, but just to be fun, they call it Mountain Dew. I'm so glad that Mountain Dew corporate is so flexible about this."

He laughed again. Like we were the amusing ones.

My daughter finally said, "You're right, dad. It's not the same. Drink away." She patted his shoulder and walked away with a smile and an amused glance my way. *I think she must have hit him up for a favor later, being a teenager and all.*

But it was so illogical I couldn't let it go so graciously. So the next time I saw him with a Mountain Dew icee, I tried again. But no amount of reasoning, humor or analogies would convince him.

The thing is, my husband is a highly intelligent man. And one of the reasons I married him was for his wisdom and logic. As the kids' grade school PTA president for several years, a coach, a ministry leader, and a successful businessman, these qualities in him are highly valued by others as well.

And yet he still insists he was off Mountain Dew for a year.

A few weeks ago, our pastor gave a message called, "Search Me." It had to do with *blind spots*.

Initially, it brought back to mind my hubby with his Dew. I started to giggle to myself.

But before I could get too proud, our pastor reminded us that *we all have blind spots*. He said that what makes them so dangerous, is as the name insinuates—we are blind to them. We really don't see them. *At all*. And yet, they can wreak havoc in our lives.

Pastor, author and speaker Bill Hybels explains a blind spot as, "Something someone believes they do well, but everyone else knows it's not true." He went on to say that the research shows that we all have about 3.4 blind spots.

And unfortunately, I'm afraid, some of our blind spots are not as benign as drinking Mountain Dew.

In Jeremiah 17:9 we read, *"The heart is deceitful above all things and desperately wicked. Who can know it?"*

And the story gets worse.

In Priscilla Shirer's, *The Armor of God*, Bible study, she talks about how Satan's number one weapon of attack on us is deceit. In fact, she calls him "the master illusionist:"

> *He pulls the wool over our eyes, causing us to think happiness exists where it doesn't, that security is offered where it isn't. He makes evil appealing and*

righteousness boring, then entices us down a dark path
that leaves us addicted, joyless and empty...

Deceit was at the core in the very beginning story of mankind. When Satan convinced Eve that what God gave her wasn't enough. (Gen. 3:13)

Jesus called Satan the father of lies and told the Jews that there was no truth in him. (John 8:44)

It is no wonder we have blind spots. We are prone to deceive ourselves in our very being, and we have an accuser trying to deceive us daily.

With the devastating consequences of deception in our lives to us and those around us, the question begs, "How do we see what we can't see?"

Pastor Bob Merritt of Eagle Brook Church posed three questions we can ask ourselves in this regard:

1. What is God telling me? Ask God to show you your blind spots and then listen. You will start feeling a nudging in your Holy Spirit of areas that need change.

2. What are other trusted people telling me? If two to three good friends are telling you the same thing, it is time to listen.

3. Where am I most defensive? This often shows an area you are trying to cover up.

Shirer also reminds us that the truth of God's Word sheds light on Satan's deceptions. Know it. Study it. And pray.

And through his Word, you will get to know Jesus, who is the truth (John 14:6). The truth of his light will illuminate our darkness and deceptions...our blind spots.

Knowing God loves us regardless helps us to take that dirty clothing of pride off and ready ourselves for a more thorough Spirit-guided examination.

So, I ask myself and God the Father, Son, and Holy Spirit today, "What is my Mountain Dew?"

Search me, O God, and know my heart; test me and know my anxious thoughts. See if there is any offensive way in me, and lead me in the way everlasting.
—Psalms 139:23-24

Am I willing to ask Christ and a spiritual friend to reveal any of my blind spots?

Flirting with Temptation

Julie

Before you make a decision, ask yourself this question: will you regret the results or rejoice in them?
—Rob Liano

If only I would! If only I would stop and give thought to my decisions. Not all decisions, mind you. In many decisions, I am quite strategic.

But, when it comes to the little decisions, you know, the spontaneous ones like, "I'm hungry, and that ooey gooey brownie would help tide me over till supper" decision, or, "That shirt is as cute as a button, and if I don't get it now, it may not be here the next time I come" decision.

Those are the types of decisions that trip me up time-and-again.

When I'm hungry or flirting with temptation in my favorite clothing shop, I fare rather poorly.

It's hard to admit, but I can be rather impulsive at times. Without careful thought or planning ahead, I can easily succumb to that irresistible urge.

It seems to me that Esau, a biblical character I have been spending a lot of time with lately, struggled with impulsivity too. Listen in to the following conversation he had with his twin brother, Jacob…

> *One day Jacob was cooking a stew. Esau came in from the field, starved. Esau said to Jacob, "Give me some of that red stew—I'm starved!"*

Jacob said, "Make me a trade: my stew for your rights as the firstborn."

Esau said, "I'm starving! What good is a birthright if I'm dead?"

Jacob said, "First, swear to me." And he did it. On oath Esau traded away his rights as the firstborn. Jacob gave him bread and the stew of lentils. He ate and drank, got up and left. That's how Esau shrugged off his rights as the firstborn.

—Genesis 25:29-32 (*The Message*)

Now, the rights of a firstborn in that day were no petty thing to flippantly shrug off. The firstborn usually received a larger share of daddy's inheritance, which could set a kid up for life.

But, on that day Esau made his decision with his stomach. He'd been out in the backwoods, perhaps for days, hunting game for next week's meals. Tramping through brush and brambles, wading through streams, walking for miles, Esau was hungry. Starved!

He didn't have the strength or the patience to pluck and prep his goose. He needed nourishment now.

Especially with the enticing aroma of Jacob's stew lingering in the air.

You know the feeling...

It's kind of like when you run out the door in the morning without taking time for breakfast, then you catch a whiff of those apple fritters in the break room and before you know it, you've nearly swallowed one down whole. And there goes willpower.

Or it's like that credit card debt you've been working so hard to pay off, and then a pair of really cute boots catches your eye in a store window. Or a darling leather purse you just can't live without. And you're doomed. The next thing you know, you're pulling that plastic card out and walking away with a purchase that will inevitably lose its charms over time. They always do.

Impulsive decisions like that may give immediate gratification, but they usually leave us with feelings of regret…if not at first, somewhere down the road.

That's what Esau felt. Maybe not at first, but when he discovered that his twin brother, Jacob, had weaseled even his blessing out of their father, it says that Esau *wept aloud.* (Genesis 27:38)

When we act on a whim with little or no forethought or consideration for the consequences, the result is usually painful. Be it the loss of a father's gifts, or the loss of our girlish figure and our health, or the loss of our credit worthiness…

I don't know about you, but I need help when it comes to those spontaneous little decisions in life. Perhaps you do, too. Perhaps we can hold one another accountable and remember this the next time we're faced with a decision: *Will I regret the result or will I rejoice in it?*

Every impulse of feeling should be guided by reason…
—Jane Austen

We take captive every thought to make it obedient to Christ.
—2 Corinthians 10:5b

What decision have I made recently, where I wish I would have used self-discipline?

The Sneaky Side of Pride

LuAnn

Pride blinds itself to its own presence, but it leaps up everywhere in our lives—it has a cup of coffee with us in the morning, and it puts us to bed at night. It is the forerunner of all sins, and it makes all other deadly sins even deadlier.
—Ed Young

Pride causes a person to kick God out of the Oval Office of his life.
—Ed Young

Pride can be like bad breath…You don't know you have it, but everyone else does.
—Mike Smith

"Mom, my coach called; is that okay if I fill in tonight?" I asked. "Brenda is snowed in." "Sure," my mom replied. We bundled up and hopped in the car. As we headed out onto our windy, country roads in the snowstorm, we second-guessed the wisdom in that decision.

It was a hodgepodge of cheerleaders that showed up to the basketball game that night and not our normal squad; it was whoever could make it to the high school through the storm.

So I shouldn't have been too surprised at what happened.

For the half-time cheer, I bent over and put my hands on my knees. When a girl I normally didn't cheer with tried to jump on my back, she didn't quite clear as she should have. As most of my height is in my legs, it was a higher jump than she anticipated. So, as she fumbled into place, the back of my black skirt got tucked up with her.

And it wouldn't have been so bad if I had been wearing my usual black under attire. But being last minute, I couldn't find them in my drawers or the laundry and opted in my time crunch to not worry about it. Not a wise choice as it turned out.

Snickers ensued from the visiting team. Could you blame them? A white, pink-flowered bottom was staring squarely in their faces from a sea of black and orange. And I could do nothing about it, as the girl cheered away on my back oblivious. I don't think my face depleted of its red color the rest of the evening.

Many things happen in our lives like that little incident from my high school days that chip away at our pride. Most of them we can laugh about later, thankfully.

And it's certainly good to have a healthy self-esteem. We are God's creation and sons and daughters of the most high, created to do good works.

But pride takes self-esteem a step further. Dictionary.com states *pride* as "a high or inordinate opinion of one's own dignity, importance, merit, or superiority, whether as cherished in the mind or as displayed in bearing or conduct."

The older I get, the more I realize how many problems in our lives have pride at the root.

On an episode of the TV show *Castle,* a scientist develops this invisible suit. Unfortunately, it falls into wrong hands, and the user commits all manner of crimes including murder while wearing this invisible cover.

I picture pride that way now.

I never thought I had a problem with pride. *(Which is probably prideful in itself.)* Although I was aware of many of my sin issues, I viewed pride as belonging to people who were full of themselves, people who thought they were better than the rest of us... Someone who was boastful and liked to toot his own horn loudly. Someone who viewed herself as a double mocha espresso with an extra shot, topped with whipped cream in a large stoneware mug surrounded by Folgers instant coffee in paper throw-away cups.

Author Ed Young, in his book, *Fatal Attractions* says, "When we think of pride, most of us picture a loud-mouthed, ostentatious, outlandish person. In reality, some of the most prideful people are meek, mild, conservative, and calculated."

Yes, pride has many different tones, colors and nuances.

It can show itself in all manner of chaos. Pride is a root in a plant whose leaves are sprouting a multitude of sins and thorns:

- In one's difficulty in forgiving others.

- When we can't admit we have a problem or sin area we need help with.

- When it keeps us angry at God.

- Is a player when contemplating an affair.

- In getting ahead at work at the expense of others.

- When it keeps us from hearing constructive criticism.

- When we don't want to ask for help from others when we are physically, mentally or spiritually depleted.

- Keeps us from making the first move toward reconciliation.

- Keeps us from being open and loving toward others.

- Seeks accomplishment as a means to find all or most of one's value.

- Causes us to obsess about our looks. Or, it can show up on the opposite end of the scale—by those who see themselves as more modest and earth-friendly and become prideful in that.

- Keeps us from asking our loved ones, "What areas in my life do I need to work on?"

- It justifies. "I'm not angry, I'm just emotional... I'm not greedy, I just like pretty things... I don't love food, I just enjoy eating... I'm not an alcoholic, it just helps me cope with life... I'm not lazy, I'm just laid-back... I'm not stubborn, I just don't like change."

- It keeps us from being friendly and striking up conversations with strangers or people that make us uncomfortable.

- It deceives us. ("The pride of your heart has deceived you." Obadiah 1:3)

- Has a prayer life that is overdosing on the me-ism: "God help me... God please give me..." over the amount of time spent praying for others, listening to God and praising him.

- Paints ourselves in the best light and others in the worst, extending less mercy and grace to others than we extend to ourselves.

- Keeps us from learning from others that may have a different viewpoint.

- Keeps us from sharing the gospel.

- Keeps us from trying new things.

- Can destroy us and those around us. ("Pride goes before destruction, a haughty spirit before a fall." Proverbs 16:18)

- And worst of all, pride can keep us from a saving relationship with God. It keeps us from acknowledging someone else is in charge. Someone we should be accountable to. Or, just as concerning, has us rely on our *own* works rather than on the work of Jesus Christ on the cross for salvation (but really, how scary is that if we take an honest mirror to our heart and soul). "In his pride the wicked man does not seek him; in all his thoughts, there is no room for God." (Psalm 10:4)

I see lots of pride popping off the pages of my blue-covered Bible as well:

- When Cain turned on his brother Abel and murdered him after God liked Abel's sacrifice better than Cain's.

- In King Saul's hatred of David.

- In Joseph being sold into slavery by his own brothers.

- In Sampson with his great strength.

- In Jonah in his disdain for God's mercy towards the Ninevites.

- Pride was swirling in and around the Pharisees and their relationship with Jesus.

- Pride was buried in the juice of the apple of the very first sin as Eve took that bite. And on it goes...

St. Augustine said, "It was pride that changed angels into devils." Satan wanted to be "like the most high." (Isaiah 14:14)

"Make no mistake about it: pride is the great sin. It is the devil's most effective and destructive tool." Says Thomas A. Tarrants, VP of Ministry at C.S. Lewis Institute.

Pride elevates "I" above God and others and is the opposite of how Jesus taught us to live. (Matthew 22:37-40)

Humility, on the other hand, is pride's desired counterpart. Dictionary.com defines *humility* as "the quality or condition of being humble (modest; not proud or arrogant); a modest opinion of one's own importance."

I like what Peter Wiersby says about humility: "the authentic humble person becomes so other-centered that he doesn't worry about himself."

Proverbs contrasts pride and humility:

> *When pride comes, then comes disgrace, but with humility comes wisdom.* (11:2)

> *Pride brings a person low, but the lowly in spirit gain honor.* (29:23)

Says Tarrants: "What throughout history has been recognized as the deadliest of vices is now almost celebrated as a virtue in our culture... Yet few of us realize how dangerous it is to our souls and how greatly it hinders our intimacy with God and lover for others. Humility, on the other hand, is often seen as weakness, and few of us know much about it or pursue it."

But humility is exactly what Christ exemplified in the way he lived his life and in the way he gave it. It's what we are called to pursue as well.

Dear Heavenly Father, please reveal where pride is playing its cards in my life. I don't want it to hinder my relationship with you or with others. I don't want it to hinder all the great works you have in mind for me to do to build your kingdom. I rightly recognize my place as your creation and you, my creator, as the one worthy of glory and praise. Let your light shine through me by disrobing me of pride and clothing me with humility.

Do nothing out of selfish ambition or vain conceit. Rather, in humility value others above yourselves.
—Philippians 2:3

Therefore, as God's chosen people, holy and dearly loved, clothe yourselves with compassion, kindness, humility, gentleness and patience.
—Colossians 3:12

Pride is your greatest enemy, humility is your greatest friend.
—John R.W. Scott

Where is the sneaky side of pride hiding in my life?

The Lost Art of Civility

Julie

Civility awareness and a common foundation of considerate conduct are crucial to our future. Let us work towards not only bringing civility back in style, but ultimately making it a lifestyle.
—Cindy Ann Peterson

Put a guard over my mouth, Lord; keep watch over the door of my lips.
—Psalm 141:3

I found myself in a long line at Walmart the other day. It's one of the reasons why I find it so difficult to shop there…those lines try my patience! Yet, there I was. Stuck, like everyone else ahead of and behind me.

Let me just say that there was plenty of foot-tapping, head-shaking and sighs going on all around me. That is until one woman could no longer hold her tongue and unleashed her frustration on the poor cashier.

Nothing unusual these days. But, what was unusual was that rather than turn away wrath with a gentle answer as Solomon so wisely advised, the cashier instead goaded the irritated customer with snide remarks and sarcasm.

This only flustered the older woman further. She searched desperately for support from one of us in line, who now had their eyes diverted in order to avoid being drawn into the situation.

After she was gone, the cashier continued to belittle the "rude woman" to the remaining customers in line.

I was saddened.

When it finally came my turn at the register, the cashier tried to lure me into her tirade as well. Instead, I shared a little story with her. I told her that several years back when my sister was hospitalized with brain cancer, I spent days at a time away from my own family in order to care for my sister's three children. And, when necessary, I brought them back home with me, so that my sister's hubby could remain by her side. It didn't take long before I felt emotionally, spiritually and physically spent and, as such, I have no doubt that I said and did things under duress I would surely regret today.

I continued, "We never know what the back story in another person's life is. Yes, that customer may have just been downright crabby, but, since we don't know, it's always best to counter rudeness with a civil, polite, courteous, grace-filled response. Because the only words we can control are our own."

She started for a second-or-two, then began offering excuses for her behavior. I simply listened and walked away disheartened.

Sadly, this scenario plays out every single day. At Walmart. At the grocer's. At restaurants. Sometimes even at church.

It happens in our vehicles, too—only we use hand and head gestures and, these days, sometimes bullets to get our point across.

What has happened to civility? To patience? To respect? To common courtesy and being polite?

I remember hearing a story that Marilyn Meberg told at a Women of Faith Conference years back of what unloading our uncensored thoughts on another is like. She described it as, "verbal vomit." She said that the one who spews their frustration may feel good for the moment, but, it leaves the other person covered in their retch. Both women at Walmart carried the stench of verbal vomit with them that day. Unfortunately, when the cashier chose not to "turn the other cheek" (Matthew 5:39), we customers were left covered in it as well.

When my sons, now in their thirty's, were young, a new form of communication hit the sports world. It was called *trash-talking*. And it broke my heart when I started hearing it trickle down into elementary and middle school conversations.

Now trash-talking has hit an all-time low in the political world. If our leaders can be so incredibly uncivil and disrespectful, what role models have we left in our land?

Jesus had something to say about this epidemic of incivility…

> *You're familiar with the old written law, "Love your friend," and its unwritten companion, "Hate your enemy." I'm challenging that. I'm telling you to love your enemies. Let them bring out the best in you, not the worst. When someone gives you a hard time, respond with the energies of prayer, for then you are working out of your true selves, your God-created selves. This is what God does. He gives his best—the sun to warm and the rain to nourish—to everyone, regardless: the good and bad, the nice and nasty. If all you do is love the lovable, do you expect a bonus? Anybody can do that. If you simply say hello to those who greet you, do you expect a medal? Any run-of-the-mill sinner does that.*
> —Matthew 5:43-47 (MSG)

Paul, too, had a few words to add…

> *Love is patient. Love is kind. Love isn't jealous. It doesn't sing its own praises. It isn't arrogant. It isn't rude. It doesn't think about itself. It isn't irritable. It doesn't keep track of wrongs. It isn't happy when injustice is done, but it is happy with the truth. Love is always supportive, loyal,*

hopeful, and trusting. Love never fails!
—1st Corinthians 13:4-8 (CEV)

And then there is this great statement of Ted Koppel's that I came across recently…

Aspire to decency. Practice civility toward one another. Admire and emulate ethical behavior wherever you find it. Apply a rigid standard of morality to your lives, and if, periodically you fail as you surely will, adjust your lives, not your standards.

May we strive, sweet friends, to live mindfully all of our days. May God guard our tongues, and give us grace to treat everyone we meet with civility, courtesy, and respect…even those who try our patience. May it bring out the best in us, not the worst.

Don't let hurt-filled words come out of your mouth, only say what is helpful to others.
—Ephesians 4:29 (EXB)

Do to others as you would have them do to you.
—Luke 6:31

What "pushes my buttons?" What would be a godly response?

Overexposed

Lu Ann

I will not let anyone walk through my mind with their dirty feet.
—Mahatma Gandhi

My cheeks went red. My jaw dropped. I was probably about five when I saw my brother and his friends who were in fifth grade running through the house and outside in only their tighty whities like they were being chased by a rabid coyote. Maybe it was all the sugar from the birthday cake and the Kool-Aid.

Regardless, I went scurrying to my mom to report this insanity— *yes I was that annoying little tattle-tale sister.*

My mom just laughed and said something about boys and dares.

Fast forward to today's world. Think of all the things our children are exposed to by age five. The escalating moral decay smashing into the thriving valley of social media has made for an explosion in our kids' hands, minds, and hearts that they are hardly aware of.

Now a child goes from being bullied on the playground to picking up his phone to see that he is also the latest victim of bullying virally… Snapchat, Twitter, Instagram, FB, Yik Yak (where you can be an anonymous bully).

Over 70 percent report being cyberbullied once or twice a school year and a study confirms that cyberbullying lowers self-esteem, increases depression and produces feelings of powerlessness. (National Center for Education Statistics [NCES], 2013).

And then there are the sites that kids can access, often too easily. My sister was shocked at a morally-depraved site that popped up with a wrong key-stroke while on her child's smart phone.

Then there was the time my son developed a "headache" while at a birthday party and called me to pick him up. On the way home I learned that there was no headache and instead heard about what the grade school boys had been viewing on the computer in the basement.

And there are the pro-suicidal sites, message boards, chat rooms and forums our kids can access, and the growth of suicide pacts kids make together online.

Chat websites like Omegle, which is a free online text, voice, and video chat website that's slogan is "Talk to Strangers," are attracting a growing number of sexual predators. One of the things that is becoming common on these sites is called sextortion. The predator extorts increasingly sexually photos and videos from their young victims. They keep the child quiet by threatening to e-mail the intimate conversations or images to that child's family members, Facebook friends and classmates.

Then there is the anonymous texting app Kik which has become extremely popular with teens. Looking at recent cases alone where rape, kidnapping and even murder have occurred through meeting up on this app are heartbreaking.

And it will probably be a different app, a different site tomorrow that draws kids in like a moth to a flame.

In this growing access to darkness and depravity, it is getting harder for us to keep our children safe—both physically and emotionally.

Here are just a few ideas for ways we can help our children:

- Educate ourselves on what the latest apps are and closely monitor our children's social media habits.

- Enable the necessary filters available for most devices.

- Equip our kids with some godly fiction and nonfiction books to read.

- Read the Bible together or encourage them to read it when they reach the teen years. The Bible is wise and transformational, and our teens are not too young to be transformed by it.

- Introduce our kids to Christian music; Christian rap is growing in availability and popularity among teens (Trip Lee, Lecrae, and Andy Mineo are three of my son's favorites). The style may not be our cup of tea, but that is not the point. The key is what will reach our children's heart with the messages of God most effectively.

- Don't be afraid to be *that* parent who insists on knowing where they are and who they are with.

- Have your kids put their phones away on a certain spot like the kitchen table or hand them to you every night before they go to bed. I have a friend who says this works great. Her kids actually get a good night's rest when they aren't giving and receiving snapchat selfies and messages all night long. And they don't wake up tired and crabby. She said that at first they were angry about this arrangement, but now they actually don't mind and are seeing the benefits.

- When our kids and their friends walk through the door, have them set their phones down in the mud room so they can actually have conversations with each other.

- Make eating dinner together with no electronic devices a top priority; try discussing the high and low of each person's day. Talking about the challenges of our day can help our kids walk through any issues they have that we may have otherwise been unaware of. (Speaking about that, have you noticed how many families are at a restaurant together and they are all on their devices and no one is talking to each other?)

- Do a serious self-inventory of what you allow you and your children to watch and listen to. Have you lowered the bar? I think what many of us consider acceptable to view today would have made our grandparents faint outright. The thing is, when we fill our minds with darkness, we start to become desensitized to all the violence and perversion, and what once bothered us, no longer does. Our tolerance for sin in others and ourselves grows.

- Consider a break from their devices and all social media. A couple parents I know have taken smart phones away from their children as discipline for a week or two, only to have the kids thank them later and tell them how much they actually enjoyed the break.

- Get out the board games. Even teens really enjoy this. We have teen and family game nights often at our house. The teens even seem to love it when my husband and I join them for just a bit.

- Encourage our children to play outside or go on nature walks. Night games of kick-the-can and lightening-bug-catching on the farm still remain fond memories for me.

- Lead by example. In my case, I can be a news media junky. I value being informed about life events. But there are times I just feel my soul become so overburdened and depressed, that I shut off the news for a week or two. Instead, I enjoy the silence, the sounds of nature, or uplifting music. It refills my soul to listen to what is pure, good, and praiseworthy. I also sometimes have phone-free Sundays and do very little in the way of media. I read in the sun, go for drives, listen to Christian music, or putz on a few things. What refreshes your soul?

- Give a plethora of hugs and say, "I love you" often to our kiddos. Remind them of who they are in Christ (victorious, equipped, loving, forgiving...) and how much he loves them.

These are just a few ideas.

Be creative and consider what would work best with the personalities, gifts, and challenges each of our children has. There are many ways we can encourage them to focus on what is true, worthy of respect, just, pure, lovely, commendable, excellent and praiseworthy. (Philippians 4:8)

As Christ followers, we are all called to shine God's light of forgiveness, truth, and love to a dark world. (Matthew 5:16) When we put darkness in, it dims Christ's light within us. What we put in our brains, comes out in our life.

Let's take seriously the impact of what we and our children fill our minds and hearts with. We need to take the worlds' influence on our kids seriously and be actively involved.

Their hearts, lives, and souls are at stake.

If then your whole body is full of light, with no part in the dark, it will be as full of light as when the light of a lamp shines on you.
—Luke 11:36

Blessed are the pure in heart; for they shall see God.
—Matthew 5:8

What areas in my life need less worldly influence and more Son-light? What can I do to help the younger generation?

How I Stopped Running

Jo

*When obedience ceases to be an irritant and becomes our quest,
in that moment God will endow us with power.*
—Ezra Taft Benson

I might have insomnia. Some nights…sometimes for many nights in a row, sleep eludes me.

There could be many explanations for my strange behavior. Perhaps I am just not tired. Maybe I feel the need to organize my closets, cupboards or Tupperware drawer. (Type A personalities do this. I know; it's strange.) But more likely than not, my inability to fall asleep has to do with my reluctance to forgive someone for something that was said or done to me. Sometimes I'm reluctant to forgive myself for an offense I committed. Either way, in the dark of the night, when everyone is fast asleep, I find myself face-to-face with God. And it's uncomfortable, to say the least.

Sometimes I'll try to run from this uncomfortable feeling by watching a movie or listening to music. Other times, I'll physically run—on the treadmill or even outside. I just need to move. I need to escape my own thoughts. But chances are, that no matter how busy my mind and my body are, when I finally tire and the music stops, I still have to confront the same challenge—*God has called me to forgive, and I am reluctant to do so.*

This dilemma of my mind draws me to the story of Jonah. "Jonah and the Whale" was how it was first presented to me in Sunday school. But the story is about more than just Jonah and a big fish. It's about God and how he loved his reluctant prophet, Jonah, so much that he pursued him even when he ran. God saved Jonah from sure destruction and harm in the most unusual way…by tucking him away inside a big fish.

You remember Jonah.

He was the prophet who God called to preach to the Nineveh, home of the Assyrians. The Assyrians were reputed to be a brutal people, known to torture the people of the cities they conquered. I can understand why Jonah would have been reluctant to go there. Jonah probably knew he would never come out of that city alive if he went on his own.

> *The word of the LORD came to Jonah son of Amittai: "Go to the great city of Nineveh and preach against it, because its wickedness has come up before me." But Jonah ran away from the LORD and headed for Tarshish. He went down to Joppa, where he found a ship bound for that port. After paying the fare, he went aboard and sailed for Tarshish to flee from the Lord.*
> *—Jonah 1:1-3*

Jonah ran in the opposite direction from where God called him to go. God let Jonah run away, but he didn't get far before God pursued him.

> *Then the LORD sent a great wind on the sea, and such a violent storm arose that the ship threatened to break up.*
> *—Jonah 1:4*

The storm tossed the ship. The sailors were terrified, but Jonah pretended not to notice. Maybe he was organizing the Tupperware drawer in the bottom of the ship. But when he could no longer ignore the storm raging outside, he asked the crew to throw him into the sea. He saved the sailors from sure destruction. He'd decided that death by drowning was surely better than death at the hands of the Assyrians. He chose drowning over public speaking. (No comment.)

But God pursued him, even in the depths of the sea.

> *Now the LORD provided a huge fish to swallow Jonah, and Jonah was in the belly of the fish three days and three nights.*
> —Jonah 1:17

What I love about this story is that God *sent* a storm. God *provided* a fish. God pursued Jonah, even though he ran. Like it or not, God does not turn away from us just because we turn away from him. He uses whatever it takes to turn us back.

Jonah eventually went to Nineveh and preached to the Assyrians. And the Bible says that those ruthlessly renowned people *turned* from their evil ways and repented. God provided Jonah, a reluctant prophet, to save them from themselves.

Oh, that God would use me in a powerful way like that.

How many more days (or sleepless nights) do I need to spend in the belly of a fish?

If only I would listen and obey when he tells me to forgive a wrong that was committed against me. If only I would realize that perhaps I am the one who is reluctant.

Like Jonah, we may feel the urge to run. But, wherever your Tarshish may be, that far-away place where you think God cannot reach you, it pales in comparison to the "with-God" life that we can have here if we will just stop running.

Where is God calling me to obey?

Discovering the Blessing of Friendship

Mommas in Solidarity

Heidi

Two people are better off than one, for they can help each other succeed. If one person falls, the other can reach out and help.
—Ecclesiastes 4:9-10

Play dates are the best. The other day, all of us moms lugged in our car seats with toddlers in tow, we spread out some toys across the living room carpet, and our babies just sat there staring at each other. The ladies cracked open some sparkling waters while the toddler boys roamed the room, and in no time, it was pretty apparent we didn't get together for them anyways. Because really, a play date? Who are we kidding…more like a mom therapy group.

"So when did you introduce a second meal?" "How many ounces is he drinking these days?" "Can you take a look at her rash?" And on. And on. And on. No one else could possibly be interested in hearing about potty-training for a half hour, or my woes on how my baby's sleep schedule has rocked my world. It would be a complete and utter snooze fest, a wasted hang out, to everyone else. Everyone else, except the very people going through the EXACT SAME THING. To them, it was like finally finding a lemonade stand on a hot summer day.

How have you experienced this in your season of life? You know who those people are. They're the ones giving jerky, emphatic nods whenever you share the highest highs and the deepest lows of what's really going on, chiming in to every detail with a, "Yes! Yes! YES." Don't you just love them? When you meet these people, you can almost feel the connection, the electricity in the room that comes from finally being understood, finally feeling like you aren't alone, finally pulling back the curtain and getting a standing ovation. You walk away feeling nothing short of a kindred-spirit-kind-of-bond after all the confessing, debriefing, and empathizing.

And this freedom we feel? This sense of belonging? This solidarity? It's exactly God's plan. He never meant for us to walk our path alone. It's been obvious since day one when God gave Adam, Eve, because it wasn't good for man to be alone. As fellow humans, we're made to be transparent, vulnerable, and compassionate with each other. We're made for deep fellowship, a close camaraderie, perfect harmony. Not just with God, but with our neighbor, our family, and friend. Isolation is not our gig; but support and companionship makes our hearts soar.

Which is why I'm ob-SESSED with Exodus 17:8-13. The scene: War between the Israelites and Amalekites. And like a game of tug o' war, there was advancement back and forth. Moses climbed a hill to overlook the battle and lifted both hands in prayer holding up the staff of God. But as the clock kept ticking and time trailed on, his arms got tired. You know the feeling, those tinglies you get when you accidentally sleep on your arm. He was tempted to drop his hands, but every time he did, the Israelites started losing. Yet every time he lifted them back up, the Israelites would make a come-back and victory was theirs. So what was Moses to do?

Cue his friends, Aaron and Hur. When they saw what was happening, they pitched in with a sort of teamwork that would make Herb Brooks proud. Aaron grabbed his right arm while Hur grabbed the left (unless Aaron grabbed the left, and Hur grabbed the right… either way, semantics). And they remained in that position, holding up Moses until the sun set and the Israelites were pronounced victors.

This is no different than the hill we're standing on today.

Whatever season you're facing, whatever battle we're overlooking, whatever weakness threatens to overtake us, we need an Aaron and we need a Hur. We need someone to stand next to us, pray with us, and hold up our hands when we're tired and where, as Susie Larson puts it, "the devil doesn't know where you end and where I begin." Because sometimes, having that group of people standing next to you makes all the difference between losing and winning the battle.

Whoever that may be, find your kindred spirit. Find that person, that group, that community, and pursue those relationships regularly. Couples, find other couple friends. Church goers, join a small group. Students, study with your other classmates. Moms, set up play dates to unleash the crazy. Because introverts and extroverts alike, we were made to be in relationship, and when we refuse to step back into the shadows of solitude and we refuse to be a hermit, we'll finally find the connection and understanding our souls long for.

Who is in my circle of support? Where can I go to link arms with others going through a similar journey?

Surprised by Friendship

Jo

When you are sorrowful look again in your heart,
and you shall see that in truth you are weeping for
that which has been your delight.
—Kahlil Gibran

From weekend getaways that bring bellies aching with laughter to late night conversations that bring sleeves wet with tears, friendship is surprising.

I had all the friends I needed, until one day I didn't.

The yearbook sentiments of "BFF" and "Always and Forever" which seem oh so true when you're 18 and going away to college prove pale in comparison to saying an actual goodbye after decades of friendship when you're pushing five decades old yourself. I wasn't prepared for that final goodbye of my BFF.

As I stood by her gravesite I thought to myself, yes…friendship has certainly surprised me.

I never thought that as a grownup I'd need to call another adult woman at four in the morning because I was so emotional that I just needed to hear the voice of my friend. I never thought I'd so look forward to a coffee date with another mom with whom I shared so much in common—from parenting philosophies to prayer, favorite books to beloved vacation spots. This friendship journey has taught me a lot about the complexities of a relationship with another human being, and has taught me even more about myself.

As a woman who struggles with what I have often termed "stubborn self-sufficiency," I didn't know how much I'd crave the input of another (who would also put herself in the self-sufficient camp). I didn't know how hard it would be to go back to figuring things out on my own after I'd had the luxury of a close comrade who was willing to put aside her own worries, doubts and problems in order to help me figure out mine.

I didn't know that walking through my house would bring me sweet memories that stung more than they comforted, stopping to peruse drawers she'd helped me organize and cookbooks she'd encouraged me to buy. I had to find a new place to sit with the Lord in the morning because all the books in my library brought reminders of years of book club with other book-loving ladies, and then our own coffee-date-private-book-club when the other book-loving ladies became too busy to ever show up having read the actual story.

I didn't know that my heart would ache as I tucked my own kids in bed knowing that hers would go untouched by their mama...the woman who first showed me how to swaddle my newborn, how to pump and store breast-milk, how to get multiple things done while my sweet babies slept, and how to parent through each stage of this wonderful journey of motherhood. And I certainly didn't know how much I would need someone during those times in life where stubborn self-sufficiency would fail me.

She held my hand through a terrible miscarriage, made multiple meals for my family during my multiple surgeries. She listened and never judged and wasn't afraid to share her own stories about the challenges we all experience as moms, wives and friends.

Yes, friendship has surprised me. This woman who thought she didn't need anyone is finding that she actually did, that she actually does, that she actually craves to be connected to another human being in a way that she might never be again.

God created us for relationships. In fact, the greatest commandment—to love God with all our heart, soul, and mind and to love our neighbor as our self—is all about relationships. (Matthew 22:36-40)

I believe that's why Jesus, himself, wept when he saw his friends stricken with grief when they thought they'd lost their beloved brother and friend, Lazarus. (John 11) Losing those we care for so deeply is hard. And, although we know that because of the rich sacrifice of Christ we will see those we love again, it does not negate the sad fact that we do not get to enjoy life with them now. The hope for our future reunion doesn't change the fact that children will have to grow up without their mom, a husband will forever be a widower, or a friend will be left without her confidant. Jesus wept, and so do I. I guess you could say this surprised me too.

My periodically-immature faith would tell me that such grief might indicate a lack of faith in the resurrection hope. But Jesus sets an example, showing sympathy for the bereaved by shedding tears even though he knew he was about to raise his friend from the dead. Scripture promises that in death, my friend will also rise and sit at the feet of Jesus.

Yes, friendship is surprising. But God's provision, care and comfort is anything but.

The psalmist wrote that "weeping may stay for the night, but rejoicing comes in the morning." (Psalm 30:5)

So today I weep, but I will put aside my stubborn self-sufficiency and rest in the knowledge that joy will come one of these mornings.

Until then, I'll continue to look forward to how God keeps surprising me.

Have I ever felt guilty for feeling loss? How does Jesus' response let me know it's okay to weep?

Seed-Bearers

Julie

It's not what you gather, but what you scatter that tells what kind of life you have lived.
—Helen Walton

It's midway through August now, and I've already spotted signs of season's change.

I've spied goldenrod blooming, burning bushes blushing in shades of pink and red, and tall grasses waving taupe-colored plumage. I've noticed crabapple trees shedding their yellowed leaves and stood gazing in marveled wonder at the peapod-shaped seeds that now top what was once a cheery carrot-orange butterfly weed.

I've been so taken by those odd-looking seed pods of late, that I've started taking pictures of them.

Have you seen them in your neck of the woods? If not, you ought to be on the lookout for them.

They're green now. But, as the waning days of summer march on, they will dry into a tanned husk and break open. Then, the seeds inside will fly.

Last year I picked a dried pod that was chuck full of seeds and placed it on my desk. I can't explain it, but, it spoke to me then... It speaks a clearer message to me now.

Here's what it's whispering...

My life. Your life. Our lives. They're fleeting.

Some of us are like annual flowers. We shine in riotous blossoms for a season…then when life comes to an end we shrivel up and leave no evidence behind that our lives graced the earth.

Others of us blossom year-after-year like perennials, faithfully brightening the world around us.

But, then there are the seed-bearers. Those that not only brighten the space they inhabit, but, who release seeds of love, joy, faith, hope, laughter, and blessing; planting them deep into the flower bed of others' lives.

That was my friend Mark Johnson. He was a seed-bearer, scattering seeds in nearly everyone's hearts that he ever met. That is why his sudden heavenly home-going hurts so bad.

When people describe Mark, one word consistently comes up: Happy. Mark was indeed happy.

He was happy in Jesus. Happy with the love of his life, Colleen. Happy and blessed to have two precious kiddos, Kayla and Cole…and soon-to-be son-in-law, Justin. Mark was happy in his work. Happy at church. Happy in life. Happy.

And he made it his mission to make others' lives happy, too.

I honestly don't know how we are going to move forward without you, Mark. Without your big heart. Your big smile. Your bear hugs. Without your seed-scattering ability to bring such joy into our lives.

But I know that the greatest gift I could give you is to be a seed-bearer, too. Someone who not only brightens the space I inhabit, but, who scatters seeds of sweetest gifts into the lives of others, like you did, my precious friend.

This is how we know what love is: Christ gave his life for us. We too, then, ought to give away our lives for others!
—1st John 3:16

I think the hardest part of losing someone, isn't having to say goodbye, but rather learning to live without them. Always trying to fill the void, the emptiness that's left inside your heart when they go.
—Unknown

What seeds am I scattering?

Sunglasses

LuAnn

*How much better to get wisdom than gold, to choose
understanding rather than silver!*
—Proverbs 16:16

Our group of close-knit friends was outside enjoying each
other's company while the sun's rays warmed and darkened our
skin, like a toaster working its magic with a piece of bread.

Finally, someone said something.

We'd all been thinking it.

"Lori. Seriously. Girlfriend… How can you handle those
sunglasses?! That one lense is *so* scratched up. I don't know how
that doesn't bother you?! That would really bother me. In fact,
it's bothering me just looking at you!"

Several of us chimed in with agreement.

Lori gave a hearty laugh as her brunette head bent back in
amusement. She seemed highly entertained, and we were baffled
as to why. Seriously. How can anyone find a severely scratched
lense anything but irritating?

"Girls, that is so funny. That's my bad eye! I can't see out of that
eye, so it doesn't bother me! I love these glasses, and the other
lense is great!" She continued to laugh.

We offered up, "Ohhh, of course!... Yes, that makes sense!" And
tried to join in her laughter.

But secretly, a part of me was horrified.

I mean really. Lori had been my friend for about 20 years. How had I not connected that dot?

Weeks later, the image of Lori with her very scratched sunglass lense resurfaced.

I was letting the dogs run in a nature area, and as so often happens, my mind started to wander. During this particular time, I was reflecting on people whose political opinions are quite different than mine. Others seeing our world so differently can highly agitate me at times, especially when I think I'm right. In throwing this up to God, he brought this image of Lori to mind.

When I started pondering that image and what God may be trying to tell me, another visual came to mind.

It was of a professor speaking in one of my communications classes back in college. The professor had said that it was helpful to understand, and even sometimes visualize, an actual filter or screen in front of someone.

He said something to the effect of, "Every message you give goes through your filter and is received through another's filter before it enters her heart. This filter can include her life experiences, the people that are a strong influence, her values, culture, what she has been taught, and her innate nature. This affects and influences how she understands and receives your message. Her filter is going to be quite different than yours. You need to keep this in mind when communicating. Our filters color—and can even distort—one another's messages."

These images got me thinking. "Maybe I need to start trying on other people's sunglasses…to see what the world looks like through her lense…his filters."

When we were talking to Lori that day, we were all picturing how *our* world would look like through those sunglasses, not how *her* world looked like. And it was completely different.

Jesus seemed to be a master at this when he talked with people. Every conversation he had seemed to hit at the heart of where someone was coming from. He seemed to know just what sunglasses people had on: The rich man that wanted to know what to do to receive eternal life. Peter who said he would never betray him. The Samaritan woman who was living in adultery. The Pharisees that thought they had all the answers. The disciples that wanted to sit next to him in heaven…

I can never understand others the way Jesus did, but maybe if I borrowed others' sunglasses more and asked the Savior to help me understand the lenses she may be seeing through...

How might I look at her differently? How could I communicate more effectively? How would my understanding and empathy increase, even if I don't agree with her? What could I learn from her that might shape my own views?

The next time I have a conversation with someone who is seeing things totally different than I do, I may just need to reach over and take her sunglasses off and put them on for a while.

"Why do you look at the speck of sawdust in your brother's eye and pay no attention to the plank in your own eye?"
—Matthew 7:3

Be imitators of God, therefore, as dearly loved children, and live a life of love, just as Christ loved us and gave himself up for us as a fragrant offering and sacrifice to God.
—Ephesians 5:1-2

What situation might I better understand if I wore another's sunglasses for a while?

Discovering God in Celebrations

Passing Over Easter

Jo

No eye has seen, no ear has heard, no mind has known what God has prepared for those who love him.
—1st Corinthians 2:9

One of my practices during Lent is to read through a book called, *The King Nobody Wanted,* an old book of my mother's that she saved from her childhood—a book that she read to my brothers and me each Lenten season when we were growing up. It tells the story of Jesus' ministry, crucifixion and resurrection. While deeply rooted in Scripture, it reads more like a novel and is responsible for much of my understanding of who Jesus is, what he did here on earth, and why he had to die so that I might be able to live.

While I certainly didn't understand it at the time, I believe my mom was reading this story each year as a way to help us prepare our hearts and minds for Easter. And now that I'm the mom, I do the same. As life swirls around so quickly, readying our hearts and minds is both gratifying and necessary.

Jesus walked with his disciples for years, teaching and training them to understand the impact of his work on earth. And when the time came for him to say goodbye, he took the opportunity to gather with them one last time, in the upper room, to celebrate the Passover feast and to remind them once again, how deeply he cared for them.

The Passover feast was celebrated each year at the same time. It was an especially holy event for the Jewish people in that it observed the time when God spared them from the plague of physical death and brought them out of slavery in Egypt. Jesus took the opportunity to celebrate the symbols associated with Passover and infused them with fresh meaning as a way to remember the sacrifice he was about to make, a sacrifice that would save us from death and slavery as well—a spiritual death and a spiritual slavery.

> *After taking the cup, he gave thanks and said, "Take this and divide it among you. For I tell you I will not drink again from the fruit of the vine until the kingdom of God comes." And he took bread, gave thanks and broke it, and gave it to them, saying, "This is my body given for you; do this in remembrance of me." In the same way, after the supper he took the cup, saying, "This cup is the new covenant in my blood, which is poured out for you.*
> —Luke 22: 17-20

Jesus would offer his body so that we could be *passed over* by the wages of sin that plague our daily lives and instead be restored to a right relationship with God the Father. He poured out his blood so that we could be spared from the iniquity that causes not only a spiritual death, but leaves us separated from God. He offered himself up for each of us as a once-and-for-all, everlasting and holy sacrifice, so that we could have an eternal connection with the One who is sovereign, who is merciful, who is always with us.

The days preceding Easter are a wonderful time to prepare our hearts. Your tradition may call for observing Lent, attending services, or giving something up to recognize the sacrifice Jesus made on our behalf. Perhaps you read through the gospels or watch a Passion drama. Regardless of what you choose, recognize that Jesus took time to prepare the hearts of his followers for what was to come. He knew how painful it would be for those who loved him to see him suffer and die on a cross. But he also knew to let them know that this would not be the end, but only the beginning of a fuller life lived in relationship with him.

And as he prepared to leave those he loved, Jesus reminded them that because of his sacrifice, this life is not all there is. And until that time when they would see him face-to-face, he would always be with them, just as he is always with us.

And surely I am with you always, to the very end of the age.
—Matthew 28:20

Father, thank you for what you did on the cross for us. Help us to prepare our hearts and minds the same way that you prepared the hearts and minds of your disciples, so that we can understand the true depth of your love for us.
In Jesus' name, Amen.

What can I do to prepare my heart for Easter?

Passion

LuAnn

At the cross the work was finished
You were buried in the ground.
But the grave could not contain You for
You wear the Victor's crown.
—Darlene Zschech

The other day I was recalling a conversation between my 21-year-old daughter and my 18-year-old son that happened a few months back.

McKayla: "Seriously, Austin, can you not find more uplifting music? This is supposed to be a season of celebration."

"Oh...okay." He tried two more songs, but when he looked up each time he was met with her wide blue-hazel-hued eyes that said, "really?" louder than if she'd spoken the words.

Upon the third try, he was sure he had found a winner.

"Austin! Seriously?!" (This time the scowl reached her mouth.)

"Mc, really?... *Joy to the World*. The title, Mc... 'Joy'..." he said shaking his head and sighing in exasperation.

"Yeah, but they need to sing it *joyfully*, not joylessly," she countered. "Or what's the point? Who cares about the title or the words?!" she said before walking off in search of better things.

Despite the fact that I was witnessing once again that my daughter will go to any lengths to win an argument, I had to begrudgingly acknowledge that she had a valid point as Austin and I looked at each other and continued to listen. Yeah, a little light on the joy we had to concede.

What the song lacked, really, was *passion*.

As Christians, Easter is the cornerstone of our faith: Christ's finished work on the cross for our salvation. Or as some refer to it: *The Passion.*

The Passion refers to the sacrificial suffering and death of Jesus Christ by crucifixion. Jesus foretold these events and made it clear that he would suffer freely for the salvation of the world. (Matthew 20:18-19)

Christ's passion…his love to the point of bleeding out his life as a sacrifice and payment/atonement for our sins.

So, I asked myself:

What is the level of passion in my response to this ultimate gift?

When I attend church this Easter, or at any other time for that matter, will God see someone who is there to simply perform a religious duty out of routine, guilt or obligation, or am I going there to commune with the Almighty God that I love and am in awe of? Am I attending because I'm passionate about learning to be more like my Father? Am I going there to be his hands and feet to his beloved church out of my passionate response to his indescribable love?

When I sing praises, do I distractedly repeat the words while my mind drifts to what I will be doing after church or mentally hashing out a problem I am trying to solve? Or, am I truly moved by his spirit and singing out of a joyful, thankful or repentant heart, *even if I am a little off-key?*

When I spend quiet time praying, reflecting, and reading God's word, is it to get to know my Creator and Savior better and hear him speak truth and conviction into me, or is it out of obligation or to try to persuade him towards my opinions? Do I let this time fill me with his passion to love him and to love a lost world as much as he does?

Jesus said regarding the Pharisees and teachers of the law from Jerusalem, "These people honor me with their lips, but their hearts are far from me. They worship me in vain; their teachings are but rules taught by men." (Matthew 15:8-9)

What is my passion level for my Savior who displayed the ultimate passion?

God said to the church in Laodicea, "I know your deeds, that you are neither cold nor hot. I wish you were either one or the other! So, because you are lukewarm—neither not nor cold—I am about to spit you out of my mouth." (Revelation 3:15-16)

It sounds like God is greatly concerned with the passion and temperature of our heart and despises any lukewarmness emanating from it. We don't like lukewarm either, really. You won't see any lukewarm offerings at Starbucks as you peruse their hot or cold coffee options.

I was reading my daughter's poem the other day, and it struck a chord with me. Maybe it will with you as well:

> A religious doer,
> A Christian conformist,
> It makes my Spirit numb and lifeless.
> Pride-filled,
> Yet church-drilled.
> On the Outside, I'm serving you.
> All the while, on the Inside I'm serving me and my empty needs.
> Walk the walk
> Talk the talk
> But with a cold and bitter soul
> Somewhere it has to stop.
> Fill up every second of every day

So, I don't have to sit with myself
in the emptiness of my thoughts
and the numbing loneliness of my soul.
Pride-consumed,
Hopeless, confused,
Overwhelmed, empty…
But…
Maybe that's okay.
The empty sighs,
The silent cries,
The consuming pride
Draws me back to dependence on Grace.
If I weren't a hopeless Cause
Then what Cause did Christ have in dying?
It is time to embrace this season—
To pray, to wait, to chase…
So, I accept this season of stillness and discomfort…there
will be no harvest without it.
Let the harvest be of no reward or honor to me, but all for
you and for your glory.
Amen

To pray, to wait, to chase…

Wikipedia describes the season before Easter—lent—as a time
of "preparation of the believer through prayer, penance,
repentance of sins, almsgiving, atonement and self-denial."

May I suggest that one of the best things we can sacrifice this
season is simply our time. To get our passion back on track, use
this time *to pray, to wait, to chase.*

Maybe you, like my daughter, feel like you are in a season of
emptiness. That's okay. What's important is that you "accept this
season of stillness and discomfort" and take this time to seek
him. God is always faithful and he will refill you with his peace
and passion in his time.

Stormie Omaritian suggests that we "come to God simply to be with him."

At Easter, what a better time to renew our passion by setting aside more time to do just that.

Seek his face always.
—1 Chronicles 16:11b

Draw near to God and he will draw near to you.
—James 4:8a

How passionate am I about the good news of the gospel?

Turn In

Jo

Be sure you put your feet in the right place, then stand firm.
–Abraham Lincoln

In talking through the Easter story with my young son, he asked an interesting question.

"Why didn't people like Jesus? He helped people. He made their diseases go away. He even raised that little girl from the dead. Why would people want to kill him?"

He asks a compelling question. What could this man have possibly done to cause the people who celebrated him and revered him as Messiah, to do an about-face—to turn on him and cheer for his death?

It's true. Jesus did heal the sick and give sight to the blind. He offered mercy to sinners and ate with tax collectors. He raised those physically dead and offered life to those dead in spirit. He loved on and spent time with those who sought to hear the truth.

Jesus was also intolerant.

The word *intolerant* has come to be known as a nasty word. The mention of it conjures up terms like judgmental, hateful, fanatical, and unjust. But while Jesus displayed mercy, acted justly, and loved unconditionally, Jesus was intolerant too. He was intolerant of injustice and oppression. He was intolerant of arrogance and inequality. And most of all, Jesus was intolerant of sin.

In his book, *The Beauty of Intolerance*, Sean McDowell writes,

> *Traditional tolerance is truly a virtue, but intolerance can sometimes be beautiful—that is, when you understand it from God's point of view. What is more virtuous than a holy God responding to sinful humanity through his tolerant expressions of love, acceptance, and mercy? What is more beautiful than God's intolerance expressed in his moral outrage toward the tragedies of poverty, racism, sexual abuse, slavery, bigotry, and other such evils?*

So, what would it mean to see intolerance from God's point of view? What would it mean to see intolerance as something good?

When we see something or someone we don't like or agree with, we tend to turn and walk away. We write someone off or decide not to spend time with them. We might turn our backs and wash our hands of them. We might decide they are not worth our time, or our attention, or even our prayers.

Jesus didn't do that. He was intolerant for sure. He did not accept the person's behavior as being something that was "right for them." Rather, he called out the sinful behavior for what it was and then he did something amazing. He turned in anyway. He stepped right in the middle of their messiness and offered to show them another way—the way where he would be more than just tolerable. He would be merciful.

Jesus turned in.

Because he was both fully man and fully God, the Jesus of the Gospels felt both compassion and anger. He preached peace and yet caused a ruckus outside of the Temple. He offered mercy to prostitutes and disapproval toward the religious establishment. This made him both loved and hated at the same time. He found himself loved by those poor in spirit who'd never felt accepted and hated by those religious elites who had spewed the judgment in the first place.

While those in power threw the woman caught in adultery in the middle of the square and sought to rid the town of such a filthy creature, Jesus turned in. He got messy. He lifted the woman's head and let his intolerance for injustice run rampant over the hatred of the crowd.

When the thief on the adjacent cross asked Jesus to remember him when He entered His kingdom, Jesus turned in one last time while on this earth. Jesus was tired, beaten, worn down, unjustly punished, and yet somehow still merciful. His intolerance for sin and his passion for sinners was so great, Jesus turned to him and said to him, *"Truly I tell you, today you will be with me in paradise."* (Luke 23:43)

This Easter, have fun with the egg hunt, eat that chocolate bunny, wear that Easter dress and gather with friends and family to honor the One who gave himself in death so that we might live. But most of all, look at those around you who do not yet know the beautiful significance of this day and the truth it communicates—that God was so intolerant of sin that he turned in and changed the tide for all of us. He made it possible for the wages of sin to be paid with Jesus' blood so that death would not have victory after all. By being intolerant of sin, yet still turning in, he made it possible for all of us to be with him in paradise.

But thank God! He gives us victory over sin and death through our Lord Jesus Christ.
—1st Corinthians 15:57

How do I picture Jesus? How does this affect my actions as a Christ-follower?

In the Garden

Julie

Do not abandon yourselves to despair. We are the Easter people and hallelujah is our song.
—Pope John Paul II

In the place where Jesus was crucified, there was a garden containing a new tomb in which nobody had yet been laid. Because it was the preparation day and because the garden tomb was conveniently near, they laid Jesus in this tomb.

On the first day of the week, Mary Magdalene arrived at the tomb, very early in the morning, while it was still dark, and noticed that the stone had been taken away from the tomb.

Mary stood outside the tomb weeping. As she wept, she knelt to look into the tomb and saw two angels sitting there, dressed in white, one at the head, the other at the foot of where Jesus' body had been lain.

They said to her, "Woman, why are you crying?"

"Because they have taken away my Lord, and I don't know where they have put him!" she said.

Then she turned and noticed Jesus standing there. But she didn't recognize him.

Jesus spoke to her, "Why do you weep? Who are you looking for?"

She, supposing that he was the gardener, said, "Oh, sir, if you have carried him away, please tell me where you have put him."

Jesus said to her, "Mary!"

At this she turned to face him and said to him, in Hebrew,
"Master!"
—John 19: 41 and 20:1, 11-16

This is one of my very favorite passages in all of Scriptures.

And I love it for so many reasons…on so many levels.

For one thing, I love that of all the places that God could have arranged for his Son's body to be lain after the Crucifixion, he had him placed in a tomb in a garden.

And that makes sense. It was, after all, in a garden that God's story with humanity first began.

> *The Eternal God planted a garden in the east in Eden—a place of utter delight—and placed the man (and woman) whom He had sculpted…whom He had formed…there to care for it.*
> —Genesis 2:8 (VOICE)

And where it all went terribly wrong…

> *The woman approached the tree, eyed its fruit, and coveted its mouth-watering, wisdom-granting beauty. She plucked a fruit from the tree and ate. She then offered the fruit to her husband who was close by, and he ate as well. Suddenly their eyes were opened to a reality previously unknown. For the first time, they sensed their vulnerability and rushed to hide their naked bodies, stitching fig leaves into crude loincloths.*
> —Genesis 3:6-7 (VOICE)

Then, in *this* garden where Jesus is lain, God redeemed that story.

The circle once broken in Eden's Garden, by flawed, sin-stained humans like you and me, finds its completion at the foot of a cross in Golgotha where Jesus died, then climaxes in this garden when he rose again.

God brought his story…*our story*…full circle in a garden.

Another part of this story that I love is God's timing. Of all the times of the year that Jesus' death and resurrection could have taken place, he chose springtime. A time when life here on earth is awakening from the deep death of winter. Both landscape and human hearts alike are experiencing the renewal of hope that this Easter time of year brings.

> *Easter is…the soul's first taste of spring.*
> —Richelle Goodrich

Then there's Mary Magdalene who at first mistook Jesus for a gardener.

I love that because, ironically, that is exactly what he is, as the Creator of this glorious world of ours.

And as such, after three days spent in suffocating death and darkness, I'd like to think that Jesus stepped out of that tomb, into that garden, and drew in a long, deep breath of fresh air, now sweetly scented with the fragrance of blossoming almond trees.

Then, spying the source of that wonderful aroma nearby, he did, as I do with my crabapple tree each spring after a long dark winter. He made his way over and thrust his nose deep into a branch-full of those pale, pink blossoms and savored the moment.

That is what a gardener's heart does.

In fact, he may have been down on his knees when Mary first caught a glimpse of him, smiling down in knowing kinship at a blood red poppy as it bowed its flowery head in praise of him.

So, it isn't surprising, then, that Mary didn't recognize him at first.

But, he isn't just the Master Gardener of creation—he is also the Master Gardener of our hearts.

And it was Mary's heart that kept him waiting there in the garden that resurrection morning…

Imagine it for a moment. Their exchange.

> *Mary's heart heavy, confused—her eyes clouded with tears.*
>
> *Then Jesus tenderly speaks her name.*
>
> *And at this she turns to face him.*

Mary heard Jesus whisper her name.

I think she could've written these words from the old hymn herself that day…

> *I come to the garden alone. While the dew is still on the roses.*
> *And the voice I hear falling on my ear, the Son of God discloses.*
> *He speaks, and the sound of his voice, is so sweet the birds hush their singing.*
> *And the melody that He gave to me within my heart is ringing.*
> *And he walks with me and he talks with me,*
> *And he tells me I am his own.*
> *And the joy we share as we tarry there,*
> *None other has ever known.*

Mary heard her name. And when she turned around, she saw Jesus. And that's when she knew—beyond a shadow of a doubt—that he was who he said he was. The beautiful Son of God. The Savior who loved her…died for her…rose for her and was waiting for her there, in that garden.

Yes! Jesus has risen indeed. And I pray this Easter you will know how much he loves you...that he died for you...that he rose for you and that he is waiting for you, too. May you open the ears of your heart this Easter and hear his voice whisper your name. May you turn from those things that weigh your heart down and lift your eyes onto his beautiful face and know—beyond a shadow of a doubt—that he is who he said he is. Your beautiful Savior.

> *See the land, her Easter keeping,*
> *Rises as her Maker rose.*
> *Seeds, so long in darkness sleeping,*
> *Burst at last from winter snows.*
> *Earth with heaven above rejoices...*
> —Charles Kingsley

How has Jesus personally shown me how much he loves me?

Bouquets

LuAnn

When it comes to life the critical thing is whether you take things for granted or take them with gratitude...I would maintain that thanks are the highest form of thought, and that gratitude is happiness doubled by wonder.
—G.K. Chesterton

I am not one to spend money on cut flowers, even though I enjoy their beauty. But, as I walked through Sam's Club buying items for our annual fall neighborhood food shelf fundraising party, a bouquet caught my eye; with white daisies and carnations tinged in black, orange and white, mustard-colored roses edged in burgundy, burnt orange tiger lilies and black statice, topped off with a mini smiley scarecrow peaking over the bouquet beckoning, "Take me home," what else could I do?

Considering my fall decorations are down to one bin and take about five minutes to set out, I knew this bouquet would add some fun fall character to our home and put me a tad closer on the playing field with my more decorating-savvy Pinterest and *Home and Garden*-type friends.

I carefully trimmed and arranged the flowers, tried out different vases until I found just the right one, and then proudly displayed them on the kitchen island, the hub of our home.

Several days later when my daughter was visiting, I overheard her ask, "Dad, did you get these beautiful flowers for mom?"

"Ah no... I wonder where those came from?" he asked.

"Dad, really…haven't you seen these before? I noticed them the last time I was home. And that was days ago!"

"Really?" he asked surprised. "Hmmmm. I hadn't noticed. They are really pretty."

Working in the mudroom nearby, the conversation made me laugh. I could pretty much visualize my daughter's eye-rolling and head-shaking.

If the bouquet had been contained in a basketball vase or had a Vikings jersey peeking out of it instead of a scarecrow, he *may* have noticed the bouquet. Then again…

But, after my laughter faded, I began to reflect and wonder: How many "beauties" do I walk by each day without noticing?

How many birds of all variety of song and color do I miss when I am working busily outside? What interesting architecture that someone has put hours of thought and creativity into do I pass by without a glance? How many people do I completely miss that walk by as I'm caught up in my busy schedule and to-do list?

When Thanksgiving quickly sneaks up behind the almost-barren trees, it is a good time to reflect…to slow down and take notice of "the flowers on our counter" that we may pass by for days without noticing. To give thanksgiving and new wonder to those blessings that have become so familiar they have been relegated to the categories of common and routine.

It can happen with people and things that are most dear to us: family, job, friends, freedoms, our health, ministries, warm home, church, and even our loving creator and savior who continuously extends grace. Wonder upon wonders.

And maybe, if we reflect long enough, we can even be thankful for the challenges that have come our way this past year…challenges that were incredibly hard, but now, this side of them, we can see how they have expanded our capacity and understanding in some manner…how they have matured us.

This is the perfect time of year to look back and find reasons to be grateful. To discover that what we often pass over or by as commonplace is really a blessing...a treasure in disguise.

If that treasure turns out to be someone near and dear to you, be sure to let them know just how thankful you are for them.

Give thanks...slow time down with all your attention, and your basket of not-enough-time multiplies into more than enough.
—Ann Voskamp

I thank my God every time I remember you.
—Philippians 1:3

...so that the grace that is reaching more and more people may cause thanksgiving to overflow to the glory of God.
—2 Corinthians 4:15

What tops my bouquet of blessings? How can I show appreciation?

Is Your Cup Overflowing?

Jo

May the God of hope fill you with all joy and peace as you trust in Him, so that you may overflow with hope by the power of the Holy Spirit.
—Romans 15:13

I stopped at the grocery store Sunday afternoon to pick up some milk. We were out again, and I thought it would be a quick afternoon errand before the big football game began. I was a little shocked to find the parking lot packed, and the store even more so. People were doing their pre-Thanksgiving shopping. Somehow, I hadn't even given that a thought yet. After all, it was only Sunday.

To be fair, I never have much to prepare for Thanksgiving. We don't host at our house, and I am only ever entrusted with salad. (I'm not much of a cook, and everyone knows it.) And lettuce can be purchased in 30 minutes or less on Wednesday night.

But for many, at least for many of the people I saw at the grocery store, getting ready for the holidays means list-making, multiple trips to the grocery store and a general feeling of hurriedness. The stress of inviting family and putting together a big meal can be overwhelming and even crippling. Those doing the shopping and preparing are often exhausted while the rest of us show up with our salads and take our seat at the table. Happy Thanksgiving!

So, this Thanksgiving, I offer a word for our hosts. Since your Sabbath day has already been compromised with a trip to the grocery store, I pray that you will find a few hours this week to rest. I know, I know, there is much to do. But for the sake of those responsibilities, I pray that you will find time to rest. It's not my idea. I am borrowing it from God.

In fact, God thought it was so important, that he actually commanded people to rest. He called it the Sabbath. It was a time to forsake our responsibilities of work and life so that we could spend some time with him. Sabbath was meant to be a time to renew, to fill-up, and to restore from the busy week of work and stress. It was also meant to be a time to ready ourselves for the potentially stressful times ahead…like a Thanksgiving feast.

There is a beautiful Jewish ceremony that symbolizes what it means to see Sabbath Rest as an opportunity to replenish and restore. It's called the *Havdalah*. During part of the ceremony, the people place a cup on a saucer and fill it until the liquid not only fills the cup but overflows into the saucer beneath. It is meant to signify the importance of filling our own cup first, with the replenishing work of the Sabbath, so that we can live our lives in the upcoming week from a place of overflow. Because then, if my cup is full, then I will have sufficient fuel to give away to others, helping them to jump-start their own efforts. The alternative is to start the week with a half-empty cup, quickly depleting your supply in an effort to please others. Sabbath rest is to allow you to start from a place of fullness, to start from a place of peace, because you've set aside the time to let God fill your cup to the full. From that place, you can accomplish all of the upcoming responsibilities.

So, if you are hosting, take some time to fill your cup—however that works best for you. It could be a time of prayer, a long walk, listening along to inspirational music, or just spending time alone in God's Word. Start with a full cup on Thursday morning, so that when the doorbell rings and the chaos ensues, God's blessings so naturally spill out from your cup that you hardly notice any is missing. And if you're lucky, others will add some of their own blessings to your cup with hugs, thank you's and offerings (even salads) to your special feast.

God offers us this time of rest so that he can restore us. Don't miss it. Add it to your list if you need to. But don't pass it by. It is as important as the gravy, the cranberries, and the pumpkin pie. Rest. Restore. Replenish. Repeat.

The Jewish people have a beautiful blessing they speak during the Sabbath. *Shabbat Shalom*. The loose translation is *Sabbath Peace*. But the more complete translation reads, *May God be in your rest, may you find God in your rest, and may you find rest in God alone*.

Shabbat Shalom to all of you this Thanksgiving.

What will I do to refill my cup for upcoming celebrations?

Seeing Christmas Through the Eyes of a Child

Heidi

Jesus said, "Let the little children come to me, and do not hinder
them, for the kingdom of God belongs to such as these."
—Mark 10:14

My toddler was a tiny one-year-old last Christmas, fascinated
only by the basics—staring at the lights on the tree, rearranging
ornaments, and thrashing around wrapping paper.

This year Oscar is two, and things are obviously different. He
wonders why Rudolph's nose is red and laughs when Frosty
says, "Happy birthday!" instead of "Merry Christmas." And he's
not only preparing for his very first Christmas pageant, but he
doesn't chew on the manger scene anymore either. Instead, he
places the angel correctly above the stable and hums, "Away in
the Manger" while rocking pretend baby Jesus in his arms.

Even though Oscar experienced Christmas last year, his ever-
growing mind soaks up all the songs, stories, decorations, and
lights like it's new this time around too. In a way like
everything's fresh. And the awe in his eyes is plain for all to
see—showcasing just how captivating and extremely interesting
every detail is.

So today I thought, "Why not?" and pulled out his doodle mat
during lunch and drew out what I titled, "The Salvation Story." I
made three guys in the sky: God, Jesus, and the Holy Spirit, with
a large arrow pointing down to a manger. Then, I drew a *t*
sticking up from the ground, simply saying how Jesus grew up
and died on the cross, with another large arrow pointing back up
to heaven. Because of course, Jesus' story has a happy ending;

he came back to life, reunited again with his Dad, and can live in our hearts and our home today if we want him to.

While my crayon was scribbling out the story, Oscar smiled at the manger, and with his sweet, pudgy arms, rocked baby Jesus. He nodded at the cross. He pointed out the window and up to the sky when we got to the part about Jesus returning to heaven. And at the end, he clapped for him, repeating my emphatic words, "Praise Jesus."

Childlike faith is really something, isn't it?

This two-year-old was mesmerized by every detail of the Christmas story. Beaming at the manger. Singing praises to Jesus. Focused on the red crown of thorns I drew on Jesus' head. And cheered Jesus on for having the power to come back to life.

I just kind of stared at him across the table. To be honest, I was a little taken aback at his engagement and pretty surprised over his delight in what (I thought) was a complicated story. And like so many moments in this whole parenthood thing, it made me stop and give *myself* a heart check.

When's the last time I was mesmerized by the Christmas story? As someone who grew up in a Christian home, I heard about Jesus' birth every year at church, at family gatherings, and during bedtime stories—and over the years, to be honest, I've started to glaze over some of the details.

When's the last time I broke out into song, giving praise to God, not just at church, but simply because I saw a manger scene? And is there a difference between the amount of passion I sing Rudolph the Red-Nosed Reindeer and Jingle Bell Rock with carols that actually mention Jesus?

And when's the last time I really concentrated on the cross and recognized the pain Jesus went through to save me from my sins? When I audibly cheered on my Savior because he rose from the dead, and without hesitating, responded with a, "Praise Jesus"?

Childlike faith really *is* something. And thanks to a lesson from my toddler, I'm reminded today it's also worth recognizing, listening to, and drawing out in others—and in ourselves. This Christmas, we have an opportunity to either blur through the holiday parties, the gift exchanges, and the traditions without looking upwards. Or we have the chance to take in every detail as if it were fresh and new, mesmerized by the true reason for the season, and celebrating in awe of what Christ did for us.

Childlike faith is not just for the toddlers of our world—but a call for every believer, young and old, new or seasoned in the faith…for you and me.

May at the end of the day and at the end of this season, we all say just as emphatically and passionately as a child: *Praise Jesus.*

How will I live my moments this December?

A Bold Ambassador

Jo

He who sings prays twice.
–Unknown

One of my favorite Christmas traditions is singing the many Christmas carols. As part of a caroling group, I have sung these tunes countless times in my youth, and now they remain fixed in my memory and etched on my heart. When I'm decorating my house for Christmas, or baking up Christmas goodies, those songs seem to spill out of my mouth without warning, much to the amusement of my family members. One of those songs spilling out today is, *Go Tell it on the Mountain.*

In 1865, choral director, educationalist and songwriter, John Wesley Work Jr. wrote the lyrics to *Go Tell it on the Mountain,* and over the years it has been sung and recorded by many gospel and secular performers. The reason I love this particular carol is because the chorus not only celebrates the Nativity of Jesus, but it also instructs us to go and tell others the amazing news that Jesus Christ is born.

Singing this song made me wonder, am I doing what the song instructs? Am I "telling it on the mountain," this amazing news that not only is Jesus Christ is born, but that he is alive and active in you and me? Do I tell others the story of how my life is forever changed because I follow him as my Lord?

This means that anyone who belongs to Christ has become a new person. The old life is gone; a new life has begun! And all of this is a gift from God, who brought us back to himself through Christ. And God has given us this task of reconciling people to

him. For God was in Christ, reconciling the world to himself, no longer counting people's sins against them. And he gave us this wonderful message of reconciliation. So, we are Christ's ambassadors; God is making his appeal through us.
(2 Corinthians 5:17-20, NLT)

We, as followers of Christ, are keepers of the story of how Jesus Christ was born. We have his story fixed in our memories and etched upon our hearts. And as such, the story of how he lived, how he sacrificed his life for our sins, and how that sacrifice reconciled us back to God, is a story that needs to be told. We are ambassadors of his story, and God is making an appeal through you and me.

I admit, sometimes I hum my carols to myself; I keep the joy I feel contained within the four walls of my house or the closed-up windows of my car. I praise God with my songs, but I have a feeling he wants that joy I feel to spill out, maybe even overflow. He wants me to go and tell it on the mountain. He wants others to hear the good news of this season too. The good news of Christmas is not just the yummy treats, the beautiful decorations and the lefse (a God-ordained delicacy for sure). The good news of Christmas is the story of his birth, of his work on this earth, and of his deep love for us all.

So read these lyrics and sing them out loud if you wish. Take time this Christmas season to tell people why this holiday is so important to you—how being a follower of Christ makes a difference in your life, and how they can experience a new life of their own by placing their trust in him. Merry Christmas my friends!

Go tell it on the mountain
Over the hills and everywhere
Go tell it on the mountain
Jesus Christ is born

Down the lonely manger
The humble Christ was born
And God sent salvation
That blessed Christmas morn

While shepherds kept their watch
O'er silent flocks by night
Behold throughout the heavens
There shown a holy light

How can I spread the good news this season?

Blue Christmas

LuAnn

Lights upon the tree
But there's no laughter in this house
Not like there used to be
There's just a million little memories
That remind me you're not here
It's just a different kind of Christmas this year...
There's one less place set at the table
One less gift under the tree
And a brand-new way to take their place inside of me
I'm unwrapping all these memories
Fighting back the tears
It's just a different kind of Christmas this year
Just because you're up in heaven, doesn't mean you're not
near...
It's just a different kind of Christmas this year
—Mark Schultz

I remember the first Christmas without my dad. I was nineteen, and it was six months earlier that cancer had ravaged through my father's body doing its final work and stealing him from us.

To be honest, I don't really remember that Christmas very well. But, I do remember the feeling. And it wasn't a good one. It felt wrong. Off-kilter. Even though my dear mom tried her hardest to make it a joyous time for all us kids. And as nice as it was for the rest of us to be together, it was still hard. I missed my dad who would wear his knit Packers cap indoors and be even more goofy than usual during the Christmas season. His presence was missed.

Is this where you find yourself this season, experiencing the Christmas blues? Christmas movies, carols, presents, the tree with its baubles, lights and ribbon, that usually bring merriment, and the treats and food that should taste scrumptious, all fall flat.

You see Christmas cheer and joy swirling around you, but that is where it stays. Outside. The beautiful, bright, winking Christmas lights outside that reflect blurry greens, reds, and blues off the white snow and burst light through night's frosty dark curtain, do little to bring light into the darkness inside your soul. Like the lighted reindeer displays frozen to the ground, you feel frozen as well.

And maybe the pain you feel isn't from a death of a loved one, but from another kind of loss, a death of sorts: A death of a relationship. A wayward child that has broken all contact. A loss of health. A loss of feeling safe. Pain can come in many forms. They are all losses to be mourned.

Each of us, if we traverse this world long enough, will experience a blue Christmas. We live in a fallen world. Those feelings are normal and okay.

One of the things I love about my Aunt Betty's pastor is how he does not minimize death and the pain and destruction it leaves behind. A pastor of a small country church in Paint Creek valley outside my hometown, I have heard him officiate two funerals, and he was gracious enough to give my aunt a copy of his notes. Here are just a few of Pastor Kenneth Kimball's thoughts below I want to share with those of you experiencing a blue Christmas.

> *People mean well when they say of someone who died that "death was merciful" but it is the language of pagan despair and unbelief that tries to make a friend of death, and death is no friend but an implacable enemy.*

Instead of drawing upon the pagan desperation of our old sinful selves in the futile effort to draw a smiley face on death, let us turn rather to the truth of God's Word and see death for what it really is.

St. Paul calls death the last enemy. Biblically, death is not simply the final cessation of our earthly life, the moment of our last heartbeat, our last gasping breath—death is everything that led up to that. The whole of our dying and all that we go through and all that is taken from us is death's work. All our life is lived in the valley of the shadow of death. Death, in all its forms, comes as the thief and destroyer, taking from us friends and family, draining us of life and health, reducing us to shells and husks of what we once were, hemming us in within shrinking horizons until our world becomes only the walls of a hospital or nursing home room and the bed in which we lie. Having humiliated us, overwhelmed us, heaped its indignities upon us, death finally, at the last, extinguishes the last faint glowing ember of our lives. There is no mercy here.

In John 11 Jesus confronts death at the tomb of Lazarus. The Greek translation of Jesus first emotion that death provokes in Jesus is anger, followed by agitation—Jesus is fighting mad at death. And then He weeps with grief. Jesus then walks up to the rock covered tomb—and again the Greek states that He snorts with anger and wrath. And then follows His undoing of death—restoring Lazarus, already four days into decay, to life.

Jesus, who is the Resurrection and the Life, hates death, is angered by death, and grieves at what death does to us whom he loves. If God Incarnate experiences anger and gets fighting mad at death, then it is okay that we get mad and angry with death too. We shouldn't pretend that death is a mercy or natural and that we have to find some good in it. We should see death, whether short or long in the dying, as the enemy.

It is when we have unmasked death for the terrible enemy it is, that we can, by the power of the Holy Spirit and the Word, now truly see who is our deliverer, our rescuer, our Savior—the Lord Jesus Christ, God Incarnate… The great news, the Gospel, is that Jesus Christ has defeated death, sin, and the devil. Jesus has so utterly defeated death our enemy as to make death the doorway home to eternal life. Having borne the weight of human sin and God's judgment, Jesus pressed on to grapple with death itself; and death, thinking it now had hold of Jesus, realized too late that Jesus came precisely for this. (Romans 3:23; 5:8; 6:3-5; 14:9; John 6:38-40; Titus 3:4-7; Philippians 3:20-21)

And it all started in a manger. Jesus' conquering of death and loss—our enemy—all began here. An almighty, powerful God, stripped himself of his power to become a helpless baby. What love can that be?! Let your hurting heart grasp and feel the power of that love.

Christmas. The reason we celebrate. The manger. The season that births hope.

Hope in knowing our loved ones that have trusted Christ and his saving work are in the arms of Jesus in a glorious place where there is no longer any tears or pain. Hope in knowing we will all be together some day because of his gift to us by coming to earth as a baby to begin his death-conquering journey. Hope in knowing that Jesus walks beside us in our sorrow. Hope in knowing that God is a restorer of broken relationships. Hope in knowing that God is our healer. Hope in knowing that God is our refuge in times of trouble…in times when we have the Christmas blues.

Christmas may feel different this year. Even sad and painful at times. My prayer for you, as one who has also traveled this road, is that your wounded heart may find some joy, peace, and hope in the manger… That God's presence brings you peace. That you find yourself spending precious time amongst loved ones that remain with you on this journey, making new—albeit different—memories.

There is hope to be unwrapped amongst the ashes of our pain because of this very season of Christmas. It all began in a manger.

The two stood facing each other. God robed in light, each thread glowing. Satan canopied in evil, the very fabric of his robe seeming to crawl.
Satan rose slowly off his haunches. Like a wary wolf, he waked a wide circle towards the desk until he stood before the volume and read the word: Immanuel.
"Immanuel?" He muttered to himself. "God with us?" The hooded head turned squarely toward the face of the Father. "No. Not even you would do that. Not even you would go so far. The plan is bizarre! You don't know how dark I've made the Earth. It's putrid. It's evil. It's…"
"It is mine," proclaimed the King. "And I will reclaim what is mine."
"Why?" Satan asked. "Why would you do this?" The Father's voice was deep and soft. "Because I love them."
—Max Lucado

Am I able to feel God's love this season despite my circumstances?

Christmas Memories

Julie

These people we once knew are not just echoes of voices that have years since ceased to speak, but saints in the sense that through them something of the power and richness of life itself not only touched us once long ago, but continues to touch us still.
—Frederick Buechner

It happens every Christmas. I get nostalgic.

Perhaps it's the music.

Whenever those old familiar carols play, sweet memories come flooding over me...like the year that my family decided to surprise my grams and gramps in Pennsylvania with an unexpected Christmas visit.

I can still remember it like it was yesterday.

Scurrying around the house like Christmas mice in the darkness of the early morning hours, packing the car with gifts, travel games and suitcases. It was such delicious fun!

When the long stretches through Indiana and Ohio began to curb even a child's enthusiasm, we broke the monotony by singing. Dad taught us how to harmonize so we could sing in four parts; my sis sang the melody, I sang alto, mom baritone and dad sang bass. It was amazing how fast time flew by singing every Christmas carol and jingle you can think of.

By the time we reached the Pennsylvania border it was snowing. Heavily. Snowflakes as big as quarters fell from the sky. The tree branches were laden with snow, creating white arches over the road for us to pass under. I was sure we had entered *Winter Wonderland*.

When we finally reached my grandparents' house, we tiptoed as quietly as we could up to the front door and began singing the Christmas songs we had practiced over the many miles. As soon as my gramps heard us, he made a beeline for the kitchen to load up a plate of Christmas goodies and opened the door, fully expecting to see the neighbors out caroling.

I can still see the look on his face. Tears shimmered in his eyes...and our eyes too.

Whenever I hear those old familiar carols play, my mind wanders back to *Winter Wonderland*...to Pennsylvania...to the look on my sweet grandpa's face...and tears shimmer in my eyes still.

Perhaps it is the music...

But, then again, it might be the scent of Christmas cookies wafting in the air.

Just one whiff of Christmas cookies in the oven triggers memories of days long past when my mom, sis and I used to whip up batches of cookies, with hysterical giggling sprinkled in for good measure. Or the years spent in my mother-in-law's warm, cozy kitchen where a tradition of Christmas cookie-baking took root and continues still, though she now bakes cookies in heaven with Jesus.

Perhaps it's the scent of Christmas cookies...

Or maybe it's snow on the ground.

The first heavy snowfall of the season always transports me to back to Christmas's spent sledding with my cousins...and my Grandma O. Sledding with my grandma was not for the faint of heart. She was full of shenanigans. One of her favorite ways to fly down a high hilltop was what she termed, "sandwich-style," with her laying on her stomach on a toboggan with the rest of us cousins stacked on top. Shrieks of laughter filled the air as we whizzed our way to the bottom...my Grandma O's being the loudest.

Maybe it is the snow on the ground...

Or maybe it's all that and something more...

Oh yes, it is so much more…

> *Christmas, above all, reminds me of Jesus.*

When God's love came down at Christmas.

Because of Jesus, memories are not all that we have to cling to. We who believe will one day enjoy one another's company again...with tears shimmering in our eyes...the scent of heaven heavy in the air and laughter resounding as we celebrate our precious reunion.

> *Every year we celebrate the holy season of Advent, O God. Every year we pray those beautiful prayers of longing and waiting, and sing those lovely songs of hope and promise.*
> —Karl Rahner

What memories of Christmas do I most cherish? How does the hope of heaven encourage my heart as I await that blessed reunion?

SOURCES

"A Wise Old Owl Sat on an Oak; The More He Saw the Less He Spoke; The Less He Spoke the More He Heard." *Search Quotes.* Web. 1 June 2016. https://www.searchquotes.com/quotation/A wise old owl sat on an oak%3B The more he saw the less he spoke%3B The less he spoke the more he heard/176/.

Jane Austen, *Pride and Prejudice,* (New York: NY, Penguin Books; Penguin Classics edition December 31, 2002).

Mark Batterson, *The Circle Maker.* (Grand Rapids, MI: Zondervan, 2011).

Arthur Bennett, *The Valley of Vision: A Collection of Puritan Prayers & Devotions* (Edinburgh, UK: The Banner of Truth Trust, 1st Edition, 1975, 11th Printing 2012).

Roy T. Bennett, *The Light in the Heart*, Web. Keep Going. 2 Jan. 2017. https://www.goodreads.com/work/quotes/49604402.

Ezra Taft Benson, Web. "Obedience – Life's Great Challenge," Ensign, May 1998. https://www.goodreads.com/quotes/15515-when-obedience-ceases-to-be-an-irritant-and-becomes-our.

"Bible: The Old Testament." SparkNotes. SparkNotes, 2012. Web. 11 Feb. 2016. https://www.sparknotes.com/lit/oldtestament/section14.rhtml.

Annie Dillard, *Pilgrim at Tinker Creek.* Harper Perennial Modern Classics (September 10, 2013).

Frederick Buechner, *Listening to Your Life* (New York: HarperCollins Publishers, 1992), 127 and 292.

Frances Hodgson Burnett, *The Secret Garden* (New York: Barnes & Noble Books, 2004), 75-76.

Michael Card, *In Stillness and Simplicity* (www.songlyrics.com).

"Cyberbullying and Social Media." *Megan Meier Foundation / Cyberbullying.* Web. 1 Apr. 2016. https://www.meganmeierfoundation.org/cyberbullying-social-media.html.

Jim Cymbala, *Fresh Wind, Fresh Fire.* (Grand Rapids, MI: Zondervan, 1997).

Catherine Doherty, *Poustinia* (Combermere, Ontario: Madonna House Publications, 2000), 51 and 55.

Elizabeth Elliot, *A Path Through Suffering: Discovering the Relationship Between God's Mercy and Our Pain,* (Grand Rapids, MI, Baker Publishing/Regal Books, October 24, 2003).

MIA FIELDES, SETH MOSLEY, FRANCESCA BATTISTELLI Lyrics © Sony/ATV Music Publishing LLC, Warner/Chappell Music, Inc. Song Discussions is protected by U.S. Patent 9401941. Other patents pending. http://www.metrolyrics.com/he-knows-my-name-lyrics-francesca-battistelli.html.

Steven Furtick, *Sun Stand Still.* (Colorado Springs, CO: Multnomah Books, 2010).

"John Galsworthy." BrainyQuote.com. Xplore Inc, 2017. 10 2017. https://www.brainyquote.com/quotes/j/johngalswo404996.html.

John W. Gardner, President of the Carnegie Corporation, Secretary of Health, Education, and Welfare under President Lyndon Johnson. https://www.goodreads.com/author/quotes/18287.John_W_Gardner.

"Khalil Gibran." BrainyQuote.com. Xplore Inc, 2017. 19 May 2017. https://www.brainyquote.com/quotes/quotes/k/khalilgibr121554.html.

Richelle Goodrich, *Making Wishes,* (CreateSpace Independent Publishing Platform August 6, 2015).

Lee Harper, To Kill a Mockingbird. (New York: HarperCollins, 1988).

"Thomas Jefferson." BrainyQuote.com. Xplore Inc, 2017. 19 May 2017. https://www.brainyquote.com/quotes/quotes/t/thomasjeff10100 7.html.

"Jesus Lover of My Soul." Web. 11 Feb. 2016. https://www.azlyrics.com/lyrics/hillsongunited/jesusloverofmysoul .html.

Sam Keen, from *To Love and Be Loved*, Shing Xiong, Bananna, Harry Tottszer. The Best Quotes 1-10. Board of Wisdom. Web. 25 Jan. 2016 https://www.boardofwisdom.com/togo/.

Russell Kelfer, Wait. Web. http://www.best-poems.net/poem/wait-by-russell-kelfer.html.

Sue Monk Kidd, *When the Heart Waits* (New York: HarperCollins, 1990), 126.

Carole King, *Up on the Roof* (www.metrolyrics.com).

"Charles Kingsley." AZQuotes.com. Wind and Fly LTD, 2017. 19 May 2017. http://www.azquotes.com/quote/535633.

Ted Koppel, Jounalist. News Anchor. Author. Web quote. https://www.goodreads.com/quotes/252176-aspire-to-decency-practice-civility-toward-one-another-admire-and.

Anne Lamott, *Stitches* (New York: Riverhead Books, by the Penguin Group, 2013), 87.

Susie Larson, *The Uncommon Woman.* (Chicago, IL: Moody Publishers, 2008).

C.S. Lewis, Quote: *To Be a Christian*, Web.
http://www.beliefnet.com/quotes/christian/c/c-s-lewis/to-be-a-christian-means-to-forgive-the-inexcusable.aspx.

Rob Liano, Author of *Counter Attack*, Web quote.
https://www.goodreads.com/author/quotes/4468347.Rob_Liano
Anne Morrow Lindbergh, *Gift from the Sea* (New York: Pantheon Books, 2003), 35-36.

Craig. D Lounsbrough, *An Intimate Collision: Encounters with Life and Jesus,* (Greenville, SC & Belfast, N. Ireland, Ambassador International, May 10, 2013).

Max Lucado, David Lambert, and Greg Dearth, *Cosmic Christmas*. (Nashville, TN: Word, 1997).

Yann Martel, *Life of Pi*, Mariner Books (May 1, 2003)
https://www.goodreads.com/quotes/12294-if-christ-spent-an-anguished-night-in-prayer-if-he.

Josh McDowell, Sean McDowell, *The Beauty of Intolerance: Setting a Generation Free to Know Truth and Love*. Quote by Abraham Lincoln. (Uhrichsville, OH: Barbour Publishing Inc., Shiloh Run Press, 2016).

Bob Merritt, "Search Me." *Eagle Brook Church*. 8 Oct. 2016. Web. 7 Nov. 2016. https://eaglebrookchurch.com/media-resources/weekend-messages/search-me/.

Thomas Merton, *Spiritual Direction and Meditation,* (Liturgical Press; Collegeville, MN 5.2.1960 edition June 1, 1960).

"Marilyn Monroe." BrainyQuote.com. Xplore Inc, 2017. 19 May 2017.
https://www.brainyquote.com/quotes/quotes/m/marilynmon498571.html.

Henri J. M. Nouwen, *The Way of the Heart* (New York: A Ballantine Book, Random House Publishing, 1981), 22 and 25.

Nichole Nordeman, *Be My Rescue*. (c) 2013 Birdwing Music / Birdboy Songs (ASCAP) / Meaux Mercy / LarryDavid Music (BMI) (Admin. at CapitolCMGPublishing.com).

Stormie Omartian, *The Power of a Praying Parent*, (Eugene, Oregon: Harvest House, 1995).

John Ortberg, *The Me I Want to Be: Becoming the Best Version of You*. (Grand Rapids, MI: Zondervan, 2014).

"Sylvia Plath." BrainyQuote.com. Xplore Inc, 2017. 19 May 2017. https://www.brainyquote.com/quotes/quotes/s/sylviaplat109981.html.

"Pope John Paul II." BrainyQuote.com. Xplore Inc, 2017. 19 May 2017. https://www.brainyquote.com/quotes/quotes/p/popejohnpa117373.html.

"Princess Diana Quotes." *BrainyQuote*, Xplore, Inc. 2016. Web. 11 Feb. 2016. https://www.brainyquote.com/quotes/p/princessdi200369.html.

"Karl Rahner." BrainyQuote.com. Xplore Inc, 2017. 19 May 2017. https://www.brainyquote.com/quotes/quotes/k/karlrahner204836.html.

Ronald Rolheiser, *The Shattered Lantern: Rediscovering a Felt Presence of God,* (Freiburg, Germany, The Crossroad Publishing Company: Revised edition February 1, 2005).

A.J. Russell, *God Calling* (Ulrichsville, Ohio: Barbour Publishing, Inc., 1989).

Saint Augustine. "Saint Augustine Quotes." BrainyQuote. Xplore, 2001-2017. Web. 10 May 2016. https://www.brainyquote.com/quotes/authors/s/saint augustine.html.

Mark Schultz, "Different Kind of Christmas." Aslyrics.com. Web. 14 Dec. 2016. http://www.azlyrics.com/lyrics/markschultz/differentkindofchrist mas.html.

Ray C. Stedman, "Song of Solomon: A Love Song and a Hymn. www.RayStedman.org. Ray Stedman Ministries, 2010. Web. 11 Feb. 2016. https://www.raystedman.org/bible-overview/adventuring/song-of-solomon-a-love-song-and-a-hymn.

Priscilla Shirer, The Armor of God. (Nashville, TN: LifeWay Press, 2015).

"Song of Solomon." GotQuestions.org. God Questions Ministries, 19 Jan. 2016. https:///www.gotquestions.org/Song-of-Solomon.html.

"Lessons in Life Will Be Repeated until They Are Learned." Frank Sonnenberg. E-motivation.net. 01 Dec. 2015. 01 June 2016. Web. https: www.e-motivation.net/591-2/.

Sheryl Gay Stolberg and Richard Pérez-Peña. "Wildly Popular App Kik Offers Teenagers, and Predators, Anonymity." The New York Times. The New York Times, 05 Feb. 2016. Web. 1 Apr. 2016. https: www.nytimes.com/2016/02/06/us/social-media-apps-anonymous-kik-crime.html? r=0.

Renee Swope, A Confident Heart. (Grand Rapids, MI: Revell, 2011).

Anne Steele, English hymn writer. Web. https://www.goodreads.com/author/quotes/527608.Anne Steele.

Tarrants, Thomas A. "Pride and Humility." Knowing & Doing. C.S. Lewis Institute. Winter 2011. Web. 5 May 2016. http://www.cslewisinstitute.org/Pride and Humility Single Page.

Justin Taylor, "5 Quotes from G.K. Chesterton on Gratitude and Thanksgiving." The Gospel Coalition, Inc. Web. 17 Nov. 2016.

https://www.blogs.thegospelcoalition.org/justintaylor/2014/11/27/5-quotes-from-g-k-chesterton-on-gratitude-and-thanksgiving/.

Iain Thomas, author of *I Wrote This For You*. Web.
https://www.goodreads.com/author/show/5785389.Iain_Thomas

Anya Tucker Media General. "Does Your Child Omegle? Predators Use App to Target Kids." *Wivb.com*. 25 Jan. 2016. Web. 1 Apr. 2016. http://wivb.com/2016/01/25/does-your-child-omegle-predators-use-app-to-target-kids/.

Ann Voskamp, *One Thousand Gifts*. (Grand Rapids, MI: Zondervan, 2010).

"Helen Walton." AZQuotes.com. Wind and Fly LTD, 2017. 19 May 2017. http://www.azquotes.com/author/24510-Helen_Walton.

John Wesley Work 2nd, *Folk Song of the American Negro* (1907). Web.
http://hymnary.org/text/while_shepherds_kept_their_watching.

Ed Young, *Fatal Distractions*. (Nashville, TN: Thomas Nelson, Inc. 2000).

Sarah Young, Jesus Calling: Enjoying Peace in His Presence. (Nashville, TN: Thomas Nelson, 2004).

Darlene Zschech, *Victor's Crown*. Hillsong. Integrity Music. 1989.

ABOUT THE AUTHORS

LuAnn Adams started her obsession with the written word at a very young age, pulling heavy Books of Knowledge off shelves and continuously pestering her mom to read. She was editor of her high school and college newspaper and then started writing for the college's PR/Communications Dept. She received her B.S. in Communications from the University of Northwestern St. Paul. After  editing for businesses for several years, LuAnn decided to start freelance editing. She feels blessed to work hand in hand with Julie Miller and her team to help bring inspiration to all who seek to know our dear Savior more intimately. When not editing or writing, you will find LuAnn being taken on walks by her 100+ lb. Newfie mix, Mia, and her side-kick, Daisy. She also enjoys connecting with family and friends, traveling, antiques and reading. LuAnn and her husband, Brent, reside in Forest Lake, MN, and are parents to two children, McKayla and Austin.

 **Heidi Anderson** is a writer, speaker, and stay-at-home mom. During naptime and the wee hours of the night when the house is actually quiet, Heidi writes the daily devotionals for Eagle Brook Church and is a contributing writer at eaglebrookblog.com. She also is a contributing author of the book *In The Wait*, a 6-week study on finding the abundant life Jesus came to give—even during a season of waiting and hardship. Ultimately, this is her passion and the fuel behind her writing: that Christ-followers would realize, know, and claim the victory God offers His people every day. Heidi was the Content Developer at Eagle Brook Church and the Pastor of Early Childhood Ministries at Eagle Brook Church's Blaine

campus as well. She is an alumnus of University of Northwestern, St. Paul where she studied Marketing.

Heidi was born and raised in Minnesota, and currently resides in Chisago City with her husband, son Oscar, daughter Mabel, and kitty Boots. And you must know she loves Strengths Finders, the flourish of her calligraphy pen, and dark-chocolate mochas on the daily.

Jo Bender is a radio host, speaker, and bible instructor. Jo hosts Connecting Faith on Faith Radio Network, a national Christian radio network. Jo has a passion for sharing the truth of God's Word and for helping others understand the power and purpose they possess as followers of Christ. Jo lives in the Twin Cities with her husband and two sons.

Julie Miller has been inspiring children, youth, and women as a speaker, teacher, silent retreat leader, author and mentor for over 30 years. She is a certified Spiritual Director and the owner of Heart Matters Publishing Company. Julie draws on her wide range of life experiences, humor and love of God's Word and His creation for her writing. When she is not writing, you will find her absorbed in a good book, puttering in her garden or dreaming of France. Julie and her husband live in White Bear Lake and are the parents of two grown sons.

OTHER HEART MATTERS PUBLISHING BOOKS

Whispers of God's Grace
Journeying Mercies
Inspired to take the Road Less Traveled
Glimpses of God

Whispers of God's Grace When we bring our requests to God, sometimes we'd like Him to respond in a loud, booming voice. We want to be sure we hear Him. We go on with the business of our lives hoping that we will recognize His voice amidst the many attractions and duties clamoring for our attention. But what if God choses to speak softly? Like the prophet, Elijah found, when God chose to speak to him in a whisper. Perhaps it is His way of getting us to slow down? Maybe it is His way of getting our attention?

Rather than fight to be the loudest, God sometimes chooses to whisper so that we must make an effort to hear. We are storytellers, and our favorite stories to tell are those that turn hearts toward God. And while everyone has their own unique story, it is through the telling of those stories that we are able to truly experience Him. In the midst of our joys and fears, hopes and challenges, we can see God there with us. Our hope is that as you read our stories, and the stories of others, that you will begin to see God in your story as well, and the role you play in Whispering God's Grace to others.

Journeying Mercies Joy and pain. Suffering and renewal. Our walk with Jesus Christ is truly a journey—one to be unearthed, pondered, and cherished. With the vision and creativity of an artist, Julie Miller pens her stories revealing the goodness and greatness of God. And through these stories, we are able to experience our own journey and His abundant mercies in an honest and authentic way.

Inspired to take the road less traveled They were common, everyday people just like ourselves. But, when the wind of the Holy Spirit swept into their lives, they were stirred to live anything but ordinary lives. With hearts wide open to the Savior's leading, they stepped out onto the road less traveled and never looked back. Across the years their voices continue to call out to us...

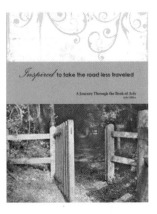

Embark with them now on a life-transforming journey by following in their footsteps in this study of the book of Acts.

To read a sample chapter of these Heart Matters Publishing books, go to www.amazon.com or www.barnesandnoble.com.

Heart Matters Publishing Company
*provides content
that awakens the soul and draws hearts toward God.*